EDITING

Best Holistic Life Magazine
BEST HOLISTIC LIFE LLC ▽
ALL RIGHTS RESERVED
https://bestholisticlife.com

Cover Image
© Alondra Vega
@alondravegaphotography

Chief Editor: Jana Short

Editors: Lunden Souza, Dr.
Dixie Short, Jessica Schreib

Layout: Jessica Schreib ▽
Jess Graphix, Germany.

Jana Short

ABOUT THE EDITOR

Jana Short is a renowned global influencer & an award winning-mindset coach. She is an NLP, RTT Practitioner, best selling author, public speaker, host of Oh, My Health... There is HOPE! Podcast, and Best Holistic Life magazine editor.

Jana currently works creating online global influencers, teaching her clients to remove blocks holding them back and how to start that love affair with their potential online clients.

She has recently been recognized and featured on the cover of the Los Angeles Entrepreneur Magazine September 2021 issue as Los Angeles #1 Mindset Coach two years in a row. Monica Garg's "Influential Women of the World-Global Influencers" 2020, Las Vegas Entrepreneurs Magazine "Top 25 Entrepreneurs for 2020" issue, and the cover of December's Best Holistic Life magazine.

Jana is getting the message of hope out into the world in a huge way, changing the world one inspiring story at a time.

Jana Short

FIRE. HOPE. COURAGE

Catch Jana on:
https://www.janashort.com/
 /BestHolisticLifeMagazine
 /bestholisticlife/
 /c/OhMyHealthThereIsHOPE

TABLE OF
CONTENT

27

Body And Health

71

Oil Of The Month

Recipes

From The Team

BEST HolisticLIFE

is looking for featured writers!

Meet
the Team

DR. ELISABETH WYGANT
@elisabethwygantwellness
Functional Nutrition Expert

DAWNA CAMPBELL
@dawnacampbell811

The Mind Whisper

DR. DIXIE SHORT
@AskDrDeeDNM

Doctor of Natural Medicine

KATIE BEECHER
@katiebeecher__medical__intuitive
Medical and Spiritual Intuitive

MARK ANTHONY
@psychiclawyermarkanthony
Psychic Lawyer
Best Selling Author

AMY GERHARTZ
@amygerhartz

A Higher Way Of Living

SHERIANNA BOYLE
@sherianna.boyle/

Emotional Detox Now

GAIL GENSLER
@Gailgensler
Pro aging fitness enthusiast

KIM HOPE
@hopeforyourfitness
Certified Nutrition and Personal
training coach

JUDY HAHN
@judybrierhahn
Functional Medicine Coach
Owner of Hahn Holistic Health

MARIAH MACINNES
@mariah__contentqueen
The Content Queen

PAULINE COX
@paulinejcox
Functional Nutritionist

CASSIDY REY
@letsgetfrigginweird
Let's Get Friggin Weird

DR. LULU SHIMEK
@drlulushimek/
Naturopathic Physician and
expert in genetic health

BRITTINIE WICK
@brittiniewick__fitness
Health Coach & Fitness Trainer
Picked Top Fitness Coach

L.Y. MARLOW
@lymarlow
Author, Influencer,.Host of Stop
Living with Monsters Podcast

NATHALIE BOTROS
@thebon__vivantgirl
The Bon-Vivant Girl

NATASHA WENINGER
@bodylovebynatasha
Author & Speaker

WILLIAM BRANUM
@William.r.branum
Naked Warrior Recovery

THE 'WHY' BEHIND YOUR MOTIVATION

BY NATASHA WENINGER

Striving to be the perfect image of success can lead to an empty life. I know best because I lived this way for many years. From a young age, I set out to try and obtain the fantasy of perfection. I told myself that once I had the perfect body, perfect career, and perfect partner, I would ultimately have a perfect life and I would be happy. That day never came because I didn't feel any joy within myself. All I felt is this incredible pressure to be this thing I thought would make me happy. I lived my life purely motivated to gain the external reward of material success and I was miserable.

It can be easy to lose yourself in the process of striving to become what society deems successful. You may have been taught that in order to be accepted you had to act or look a certain way so you could get the reward of approval. This cycle over time can affect who you allow yourself to be. Meaning you can lose track of the 'why' behind your motivation and slowly grow into someone you aren't. You might compare your level of success to others and wonder why you can't find that balance that you crave to stay consistent with your goals. Or maybe you are consistent, but you feel burnt out by the pressure you put on yourself to always stay motivated to hit your goals so you will feel successful. The reasons why you are motivated can lead you towards a deeply meaningful life or it can lead you to a superficial life that lacks meaning. The intention of this article is to offer a moment for you to dive inward to explore your 'why.' SO here we go...

There are a million reasons why we get motivated. To understand if your motivation is internal or external, let's discuss intrinsic and extrinsic motivation. Meaning, are you focused on the end game of what reward you will get once you complete your goal? Or are you focused on following your own joy during the process of meeting a goal?

For example, extrinsic motivation is all about external rewards such as love, money, sex, praise, fame, approval, status, acceptance, etc. Having some or all these things is what is perceived as success in our society and if we aren't careful this kind of motivation can take us away from our joy. My old self was extremely motivated to get love and approval for how I looked. I thought that once I had achieved the perfect body I would then be rewarded with the perfect life. However, once I realized that I wasn't being true to myself all the external rewards felt like some empty desperate search. YOUR turn! Write down how you are currently experiencing a form of extrinsic motivation?

Next, intrinsic motivation is the kind of motivation that gives you joy solely through the process of moving toward what fills you up from the inside out. You feel happy when taking intrinsic action because the desire is coming from within. You are following your own joy rather than focusing only on the outcome of material success. My motivation now looks like this: How will the goal bring me fulfillment from the inside out? Does this goal bring me joy? Will I enjoy the process? Will I be gentle with myself if I don't achieve the goal? YOUR turn! Write down how are you currently experiencing a form of intrinsic motivation?

As a self-acceptance coach, I guide women to discover what is truly authentic for them by offering deep reflection through my inner workouts. The following exercise can be used as a tool to reach your own clarity.

The Inner Workout–

Start asking yourself '**why**'? At the beginning of the week write down the tasks you want to get done. Ask yourself why it's important to accomplish each task. For example: are you motivated to fulfill the task because you are doing it for yourself? Or, are you doing it to get recognized or to try to make others approve of you? Get clear with your intentions of why you are motivated. If you see something on your list that is causing you to feel really stressed out, you may need to sleep on it before you decide what you would like to do.

The more you understand the 'why' behind your motivation, the more you will understand the internal and external process you are having with yourself.

The ultimate reward is living your life for yourself and following the path that aligns with that. This takes an honest effort from you to get real with what is not working in your life. When we crave a change within, we must allow ourselves time to reflect on how we have been living our lives. Be patient with yourself during your process of discovering where you might be stuck. If you are looking for a supportive place to discover how to boost your self-confidence and self-acceptance, I would love the opportunity to work with you. Please visit my website BodyLoveByNatasha.com to view my offerings. Also, if want to explore change on your own, I invite you to read my book, The Voice Inside, available on Amazon. The first 25 pages are free when you subscribe to my website.

Free Self-Love Quiz

I DON'T MATCH MY TOWELS NO MORE

(5 QUICK AND SIMPLE WAYS TO HEALTHY ENTREPRENEURSHIP LIVING)

BY L.Y. MARLOW

One of the things that have baffled me for more than 50 years is: how in the world did my mama feed, clothe, and raise five kids on a monthly budget of less than $500? A budget that also included rent, taking us out on a field trip to the beach, a drive-in movie, or an occasional Coney Island or Six Flags amusement park; all the while ensuring we had nice towels that hung in the tiny bathroom that was shared by the whole family.

Though a woman of minuscule means, my mama always somehow found a way to buy and hang nice, freshly washed, matching towels that represented order in our home.

I've had my share of matching towels.

Whether the decorative kind that hung like a piece of art in the countless bathrooms I'd spent a fortune on, or fluffy ones that wrapped you like a hug and made you feel loved.

Though that once represented order for me, the pandemic (and other life stressors) have made me rethink how I want to live. So I gave away or sold all my belongings (including the towels), packed up what little I needed, and moved to Panama. Yup! Hell, why not?

If I could work smarter and not harder from anywhere in the world; why not do it while sitting on a sunny beach, taking in the stress-free aroma and sipping on Mojitos (virgin of course... not 😊)

Beyond giving up the matching towels, I also had to give up my old way of thinking about how to make my life work for me instead of working for it. So I've adopted five quick ways to healthy entrepreneurship living that I think you'll appreciate too. Let's dive in...

1) Make your work fun

If nothing else resonates with you about this article, this is one thing you gotta pay attention to; but it's going to require a mindset adjustment. Change the way you think about your work! In other words, don't say: "I have to go to work".

Instead say: "I get to go and have some fun!" And also try these tactics to help: decorate your workspace to make it more inviting and empowering; take several breaks throughout your day and do something you enjoy (like taking a walk on the beach); listen to inspiring music to boost your momentum; change your scenery (maybe work at the park or a vintage coffee shop); laugh at yourself when you do something goofy or make a mistake; and above all, smile and be grateful that you're able to do what's speaking to your heart.

2) Focus on your priorities

Stop focusing on busy, mundane tasks, like checking emails and social media. Instead, prioritize three things each day that are going to help you grow your business and succeed. Ask yourself: "How do I invest the least amount of time in the most important tasks in a productive manner?" Then break down your priorities into more manageable bite-size chunks and resist the urge to try to force 30 hours of work into 6 hours.

3) Stay in your lane

Okay, I'm about to keep it real with you: stop trying to be Miss Suzy Q Versatility and do it ALL! Focus on what you're good at, and delegate or outsource everything else. For example, hire a virtual assistant to do the mundane and time-consuming tasks or use services like Upwork or Fiverr (an online marketplace for freelance services). Since you can only do so much in a day; why not use your time wisely in a way that's going to further your vision?

4) Trust your instincts

Remember, your natural-born, God-given instincts are what got you to where you are. So if something is gnawing at you, and you can't eat, sleep, or focus; and that small still voice in the pit of your stomach is speaking to you; you gotta trust it! It means that your intuition is tossing a pebble at you. Pay attention, listen, and trust it before it throws you a brick.

5) Don't sweat the small stuff

First, get out of your head and into your heart. Stop worrying about the would've, could've, should've. Quit trying to be perfect. Learn to acquiesce and let someone else be the hero. Practice compassion, gratitude, kindness, and patience. Focus on what really matters (your health, family, and peace of mind). Shut up and listen—first to your wise heart and then to others. And once and for all, stop sweating the small stuff.

Now, let's try a simple exercise. Walk into your bathroom or linen closet, grab all your towels, and throw them up in the air. That's right, give it all you've got and let them land wherever they fall; then resist the urge to pick them up. Give yourself permission to be a bit messy, go with the flow, and above all, have a Mojito 😊 .

If you enjoyed this article and are interested in learning about more ways to manage stress and find your calm during the storm, sign up below to get a guide I've put together for you: 5 STRESS REDUCTION TECHNIQUES FOR WHEN YOU'RE FEELING OVERWHELMED. Connect with L.Y. Marlow Link: https://lymarlow.taplink.ws/

5 Stress Reduction Techniques for When You're Feeling Overwhelmed

OPENING PROSPERITY DOORS: 8 VIRTUES TO ENERGIZE YOUR CA$H FLOW

DAWNA CAMPBELL

In a world of uncertainty, fear, and anxiety, having an abundant mindset is priceless for heart-centered business owners and entrepreneurs. Our mental state affects our personal finances more than you realize. One of the essential keys in releasing old patterns of behavior, and reprograming the subconscious to receive prosperity. Virtues are positive moral characteristics that enhance how we feel about ourselves on a deeper soul level that opens the doorway to abundance. Here are 8 virtues that will enhance your heart space, energize your ca$h flow and open those prosperity doors.

Peace

A calm and tranquil feeling, inner peace will help overcome any money obstacle. Peace is true freedom from disturbance or conflict over money issues and includes stress reduction. Money, abundance, wealth, and prosperity are all part of a strong foundation and stabilize the root chakra (energy center). "Having a piece of the pie" is a way to share in the profits of the business.

Balance

Having balance brings contentment and is the center point between the material and spiritual worlds. The scales have a proper distribution of weight that allows prosperity doors to balance giving and receiving. Material success can then be invited in through spiritual success. Balance is a way to monetize your creations to come through in the sacral chakra– and don't forget to balance your bank account or look at those balance sheets.

Joy

Joy brings good fortune, happiness, and the return of money. This is the fuel that is needed to properly nourish the emotional and physical body that will easily attract back successful undertakings, joint venture partnerships, and repeat business. Receiving money can enhance your personal power in the solar plexus. Think of when you received your first dollar as a child. A personal sense of worth was instilled for a job well done and a smile that is priceless.

Love

The energy of pure love is incredibly tender, soft, and nurturing energy that makes all things possible. If you look at the dollar bills, it says "for legal tender of all debts, public and private". Love is the legal tender for all spiritual debts. Love is formless energy, yet forms all things and connects the heart, mind, and finances together. Every idea and thought was first a vibration, and then came into physical form through the heart chakra. Red roses, for example, is a physical symbol of love coming into form.

Gratitude

Verbally communicating appreciation for people, environments, circumstances, and material possessions is gratitude and open the throat chakra. As appreciation increases, so does gratitude, and you feel valued, cherished, and a feeling of abundance. Monetarily, value and appreciation accumulate and increase. In the money world, leaving a gratuity for exceptional service is an expression of shared abundance.

Harmony

Harmony is being in vibrational alignment with money. Think of a finely tuned piano playing a beautiful melody. If one of the piano keys is out of tune, it will definitely be noticed. You are also finely tuned, and if your vibration is out of tune with money, people will definitely notice. Having money harmony brings in financial harmony and freedom and people will hear a perfect melody playing opening the ear chakras, rather than the needy, clingy, money energy.

Beauty

True beauty is an exceptional combination of intense pleasure and deep satisfaction.

Beauty is seen in the eye of the beholder and opens the 3rd Eye Chakra. How money is seen and viewed will either bring pleasure or complete despair. Beauty is a great reminder of nature and that all things come from the one true energy source. When beauty is expressed, infinite creations open new energy doors to receiving more prosperity into your life.

Truth

Truth aligns the inner feelings and thoughts, with outward action and opens the crown chakra. Living in your truth allows for the sincerity of action and the direct experience of feelings to validate your existence. When the truth is lived authentically, aligning with your feelings, your direct thought experience will instantly create. How you think and feel on the inside will be how the money resonates with you on the outside.

- A person who is kind will be kind with their money and receive money in kind.
- A person who is a gambler will gamble with their money take high risks for a possible high return.

- A person who is gracious will be gracious with their money and receive gratuities.
- A person who has stress will stress their money supply, constricting the flow of money.
- A person who is mindful will be mindful with their money, and money returns modestly.
- A person who is greedy will be greedy with their money, penny-pinch, and be called cheap.
- A person who feels abundant and prosperous will have opened their prosperity doors to allowing money ca$h flow in.

Take a look at your money virtues and see which ones are needed for you to have unlimited ca$h flow. If you feel less than, not enough, or any lower qualities, you are inhibiting money to grow abundantly. If you believe that you can improve your money position, then grab my 5 tips to Becoming Financially Fit here: https://dawnacampbell.com and schedule your private consultation and uncover what is stopping you from opening your prosperity doors and creating that abundant mindset.

Links:

https://linktr.ee/dawnacampbell

Money Matters

PAUSE A MOMENT TO TAKE IN THE SIGNS

BY SHEILA VIJEYARASAS

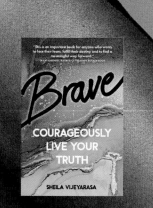

Do you receive signs? When you receive signs from the universe, do you recognize them?

Many of us receive regular signs from the universe, but often they get lost as we race through life at a hectic pace. Or maybe we do see them, but write them off as coincidence. You might notice that repeated times and numbers start showing up when you look at a clock or your phone like 11.11 am or 2.22 pm. Perhaps you're considering a career move, and suddenly you find yourself driving behind a bus with an advertising banner that relates to your new job. Signs may come when you're grieving: a black butterfly you've never seen before flies past you, the same one that your loved one was known to adore.

What can never be wholly captured by the written or spoken word is the awe we can feel when we receive the sign: the astonishment, disbelief, and sense of the surreal that ignites within us.

In those unfolding moments, hours or days after experiencing what you feel is a sign, a pattern is often altered in your life. The unique drum beat that each of us marches to slowly changes rhythm, like a new scene in a movie beginning accompanied by a different soundtrack, providing new energy and perspective.

Be Still Practice: How to Receive Signs

Here is one approach to try out for yourself:

1. Close your eyes and center yourself in your own bubble of white light.

2. Think about the issue or problem you need guidance on. Slow your breath as you think about the issue you are facing.

3. Then request in your own inner voice 'Universal Spirit, please show me a clear sign as a confirmation of the choice ahead of me?'

   Be open and receptive to receiving the sign(s). The Universe may come back quickly with a sign of confirmation, or it might send you a series of synchronistic signs that confirm themselves over a few days.

4. After you receive a message or a sign from the universe you need to be humble and give thanks for it.

Now we understand what a sign is, here comes the mini-Masterclass on how to move past the receiving, and into the integration of the message within that sign. Here I ask you to consider, what if simply noticing the sign isn't the most powerful part of identifying a sign? What if I was to tell you that it's the space and time after you've received a sign where the real magic begins?

I call the space after you receive the sign 'sign shock'.

Sign shock is the space where we inhale and momentarily stop breathing, where the logical mind tries to assert its rationality. It is the moment when our soul quickens before we dare to dream. The sign shock space is both precious and delicate. If we allow ourselves to be taken out of the awe of the experience by thinking 'I guess, it's not that big a deal, or 'we were meant to bump into each other', then the awe will evaporate along with the meaning, the information, the urgency and the instructions to follow. The sign is meant to evoke emotion but if we are stuck in the logical side of our brain, or the belief that we are too busy to feel type, we don't get to feel the magic of the message.

If we do not honor the space after the sign, we cannot move into asking the important questions. What do I do with this information? What is my truth? These are some of the questions we need to ask after receiving a sign. If we get stuck ruminating over the validity of whether a sign and synchronicity is even a thing, we can get in our own way regarding being able to walk through a potential new doorway towards personal development, spiritual expansion, or moving into action to make the necessary changes in our life.

The synchronicity of signs relates to coincidences that are meaningful. However, it is we who must be courageous enough to create that meaning. As the special recipient of the sign, we are the only ones who can do something helpful or profound with it. We must be courageous enough to keep going long after the vividness of the sign has faded in our minds.

When we get into flow with the universe, and into the knowing there are signs all around us, we get more on purpose and in sync with who we are. As part of this process, there can often be an acceleration in the frequency in which we see signs. The feeling of being authentic and following your path means that your senses are activated. They must be activated to follow your destiny. Our intuitive sense of clairaudience, our 'clear hearing', must be activated to hear the sign in another person's voice. Spiritual teacher Colette Baron Reid describes cledon as 'a message from Spirit that is innocently and unknowingly delivered to you by someone or something else. And, once you tune into the cledons all around you, you'll be truly amazed at the personal and powerful messages Spirit has for you.' So, when your Uber driver is singing along to a song on the radio, and that song speaks directly to you, get curious and be open to hearing the messages.

Connect with Shelia
https://linktr.ee/iam__sheilav

EMPOWERING
INTUITION

MOST PEOPLE DO NOT WANT TO FATALLY HARM ANOTHER PERSON

BY CATRINE BO'

My name is Catrine Bo' Griffith, and I'm the Founder & President of Life Target. I'm also a public speaker, visual artist, and the author of Life Target: Heal and Free Yourself from Your Enemy.

I was born in Limoges, France. I emigrated to the United States in the mid-1980s at the age of 20 and landed in Manhattan, NY, where I've lived ever since.

After years of self-reflection, I began expressing my emotions through artwork- www.catrinebo.com. My sense of responsibility, empathy for people, and desire to serve my community became the pillars of my non-profit organization Life Target, which I founded in 2016-www. lifetarget.org.

> ## "most violent acts are the result of emotional situations that can be avoided"

My focus is on serving and communicating that most violent acts are the result of emotional situations that can be avoided if people are given the right support.

Simply put, violence can be interrupted. I have experience with this. I was 11 years old and in the midst of a crisis that I thought I could handle alone. However, it was a situation I couldn't handle appropriately. I was on the verge of stabbing my father when a brother intervened. Little did I know, this moment became the foundation of Life Target. In my book, Life Target: Heal and free yourself from your enemy, I detail the impact and consequences of using deadly force and above all the possible healing process for the well-being of our body and mind.

I believe that most people do not want to fatally harm another person. We are all taught murder is wrong; therefore society treats the mere discussion of killing and violence as taboo. We have to lift the veil of shame on this subject because people need to understand how to assuage emotional distress that can erupt during a crisis. People in these situations must get assistance as soon as possible. If individuals who decide to inflict harm are given access to a proxy, the choice of taking a life would be drastically reduced. For this conversation, a proxy is a trained or licensed professional to help people through an emotional ordeal without it resulting in violence.

I am turning my experience into triumph by making it my mission to help people trust their inner good and encourage them to seek help in times of crisis. For that to happen, I had to create a crisis service. My main concern is to ensure that this community people are receiving the best possible support. The non-profit has successfully established Life Target Emergency Proxy (L.T.E.P.). It is a free, 24 hour-7 days week crisis search engine making nearly 500 services available in four different ways: hotline, chat, text, or online counseling.

Life Target now helps over 1,600 visitors each month, despite the complex subjects involved.

I drive the mission of Life Target wholeheartedly and invite people who have been in these situations to become more involved in helping Life Target and others going through crises. Remember, in previous decades people affected by suicide, HIV, and substance abuse were shamed and left in despair until the community and non-profit organizations provided support with the right emotional and health assistance.

This is just the beginning of this incredible journey.

My vision is to create a stand-alone 24/7 homicide hotline where people will feel safe to call and get the help they need. People will be free to express their downfalls and admit to their violent thoughts. They will not be shamed at Life Target. Here, they will receive the moral support they need while taking responsibility for discovering the leader they are over their life and freeing themselves from the vigilante they have become.

I want Life Target: Heal and free yourself from your enemy to be available to as many people as possible, especially to students to prevent school shootings. For that to happen, I am launching a long-term GoFundMe campaign called Sponsor free books for homicide prevention where people can buy as many books as they wish. This will allow the community to read emergency information and reduce the crises, overwhelming us all. Extra books purchased will

LIFE
TARGET

Heal and Free Yourself from Your Enemy

Catrine Bo' Griffith

be given to community centers, schools, universities, and distributed at street events.

Life Target is a positive outlet and a part of yourself, whether you are directly involved in such a crisis or not. Violence will never disappear as fear and anger are part of our emotions, yet we can learn how to back up from violence with the right information.

I invite you to be by my side and trust Life Target's mission for the peace that you all deserve.

Connect with Catrine Bo'
https://www.catrinebo.com

SPIRIT COMMUNICATION AND THE WHITE HOUSE

BY MARK ANTHONY

The new First Lady was overwhelmed. Her husband, the recently elected President, succeeded what many political analysts considered the worst President in America's history. The country was in turmoil and on the brink of civil war. To make matters worse, a pandemic swept through the country. The media continually reiterated how the public had little confidence this President could unite the country. As First Lady, it was her mission to support and comfort the President, but they were both grieving the loss of a son.

Sound familiar? That was the situation in 1861 when Abraham and Mary Todd Lincoln became residents of the White House.

Many talented women have served as First Lady, and being criticized comes with the territory. In recent history, Nancy Reagan, Hillary Clinton, and Melania Trump were frequent targets for the press, but no First Lady has been dragged through the mud like Mary Todd Lincoln. She died 140 years ago this month on July 16, 1882. I believe it's time for another look at America's most controversial First Lady.

Mary Todd came from a wealthy Kentucky family. Highly educated and fluent in French, her family felt Abraham Lincoln was beneath her station. Nonetheless, they married. Sadly, a few years later in 1850, their four-year-old son Edward died of tuberculosis.

The grieving parents grew closer. With Mary at his side, Abraham pursued a political career which landed him in the White House. Hailing from Illinois they were neither genteel Southerners nor cosmopolitan Northerners. Washington society regarded them as hicks. When First Lady Lincoln redecorated the White House, the media called her overly lavish and garish. When the Civil War broke out, early Confederate military successes degraded Lincoln's popularity. Then in 1862, their favorite son, eleven-year-old Willie Todd Lincoln died of typhoid. To us, the Lincolns are historical figures. But they were also parents who lost two children.

Mired in grief the President didn't go to work for a week. Mary spiraled into depression. Questions about her sanity permeated the press.

Mary Todd Lincoln was a devout spiritualist. She enlisted the services of Nettie Colburn Maynard, one of the most reputable psychic mediums of the time. On April 4, 1863, Nettie Colburn Maynard conducted the first of eight spirit communication sessions for the First Lady at the White House. President Lincoln even attended the first one. Receiving messages from her loved ones in spirit comforted Mary. Even though these sessions were conducted with the utmost secrecy, this juicy gossip was leaked by White House staffers to the press.

According to the newspapers it was now official—Mary Todd Lincoln was insane, thought she talked to ghosts, and conducted secret séances at the White House.

The woes of the First Lady were far from over. On April 14, 1865, just days after the Union victory, President Lincoln was shot in the head in the seat next to Mary at Ford's Theater in Washington D.C. Mortally wounded he was rushed across the street to the Petersen House where the First Lady watched her husband die. Six years later, in July 1871 tragedy struck Mary again when her eighteen-year-old Thomas "Tad" Lincoln died of tuberculosis. She had now lost three of her four sons.

For the rest of her life, Mary Todd Lincoln was ridiculed by the press for her spiritual beliefs. Nevertheless, she remained a devout spiritualist. She shared this devotion with another grieving widow across the Atlantic—Queen Victoria whose beloved husband Prince Albert had died of typhoid. Bonded by grief, the Former First Lady and the Queen wrote to each other frequently. Although Queen Victoria was treated respectfully by the British press, rumors circulated about her association with mediums. Intense grief is often confused with mental illness. But grief is a path no one wants to take but one we're all forced down at some point in life. For many people, spirit communication is comforting because it provides evidence of the continuity of life beyond death.

My life's mission as a psychic medium is to facilitate communication for people with their loved ones in spirit. I've conducted thousands of readings, many for bereaved parents. My latest book, "The Afterlife Frequency: The Scientific Proof of Spiritual Contact and How That Awareness Will Change Your Life," explains in an easy-to-understand way how spirit communication is real and based on sound scientific principles. It also demonstrates how spirit communication is an important healing step in the journey through grief. Mary Todd Lincoln has been treated very unkindly by history. She lost three sons. Her husband was President during the Civil War while her brother fought for the Confederacy. She witnessed her husband's murder. She was relentlessly ridiculed and labeled insane by the press. And to top it off she was going through menopause!

Mary wasn't insane. She turned to spirit communication as a means of coping with grief during a time it was clandestine, if not taboo. Now it is openly practiced and studied by scientists. If anything, she was a courageous spiritual pioneer way ahead of her time.

Can we possibly give this First Lady a break?

Oh, and by the way...the spirit of Abraham Lincoln has been spotted at the White House by several very credible sources ranging from President Teddy Roosevelt to British Prime Minister Winston Churchill to members of the Reagan family and beyond. But that is a story for another time...

Get Your Copy Today

Mark Anthony, JD Psychic Explorer® (aka The Psychic Lawyer) is a fourth-generation psychic medium and Oxford-educated trial attorney. Mark travels to mystical locations in remote corners of the world to examine Ancient Mysteries and Supernatural Phenomena. Mark Anthony is a columnist for Best Holistic Life Magazine and the author of THE AFTERLIFE FREQUENCY. His other best-sellers are NEVER LETTING GO and EVIDENCE OF ETERNITY.

WHAT THE HECK IS A INFLUENCER ANYWAY? IT'S YOU!

BY JANA SHORT

Whether you are a lover of sports, fashion, music, or business, you tend to follow some professionals who have carved a niche for themselves on your social media platforms, especially Instagram, by garnering huge followers and gaining momentum. Such individuals create experiences that impact our actions and decisions, hence the name 'influencer.'

Do you know you have been influencing others all your life? If you don't think so, why do you think some people follow you on your social media handles? Or why are they always eager to see your informative post? Of course, they see you as affecting them in one way or the other.

The most popular type of influencer is the social media influencer.

> *Do you know you have been influencing others all your life?*

What influencers do

Was there any time you got to buy a product or service through the recommendation or approval of someone you follow, probably a celebrity? I mean, someone who stands a good chance to influence a significant portion of their audience just by mentioning a particular product or service.

You remember, right? Why did you buy the product mentioned by such an individual? Of course, you not only look up to them but also trust them to help you make sound buying decisions.

This is how influencers tweak the emotions of their audience. Advertisers approach them and ask them to help promote a product or service. They then create a story that aligns with the promotion. By sharing their personal experiences with the product or service, they would have depicted a great sense of authenticity that inspires their followers to either purchase or promote such a product or service.

You still don't consider yourself an influencer?

Come to think of this. When you make a post on Facebook, for instance, that requires people to form an opinion, you tend to see some of your followers being driven into a discussion which may lead to different opinions.

Just like professional influencers, you also post memes, the food you eat, the trips you make, and other activities you engage in - but you were not probably paid for it. It is not to say that all professional influencers on social media get paid.

While you may not always change people's opinions, the fact that you motivated them to engage with your post qualifies you as an influencer. Apart from engaging with your post, they may also share it with their loved ones and get them hooked to your post. Then the chain continues - and before you know it, you're already building a brand, whether knowingly or unknowingly.

Let's take it off social media

Consider this scenario.

You are thinking of acquiring a personal computer and immediately you considered the thought, the first person that came to your mind was Rose, a computer expert who owns a cyber cafe.

Of course, it is expected that she would have a variety of computers in her shop. Beyond this, she took a special interest in learning about various brands and models as well as the local shops that sell the most reliable brands.

You could also remember how much she'd pressurized you to acquire a personal computer to make your freelancing work easier. For this, you'd have established a high level of trust in her, rather than a random shop owner who sells computers and would always 'talk' you into buying from them even when you're not comfortable with the idea.

Little did Rose know that she was already an influencer in your decision to purchase a computer. Obviously, what motivated her to learn more about computers was her passion and the need to possess reliable computers to aid her business.

It is this same passion that positioned her as an expert, which motivated your decision to trust her. The next thing, probably, for her is to monetize such knowledge and experience sharing.

Just like Rose, there are a lot of people out there that serve as a repertoire of knowledge. People come to them to seek advice or opinion that will inform their decision or action. They are what I'd call 'subtle influencers.'

Never lose the chance

Here, I'll spell out some signs that qualify you as an influencer.

Whether at school or at work, have you ever been in a place where you have this go-to person who tends to keep a tab on occurrences and people seek them to get credible information? Call them a gossiper. As long as they do not distort what they know or spill out everything they know without discernment, they could be regarded as an influencer. If you're such an individual that wants to be at the center of information flow, then you're a potential influencer.

Do you have knowledge of a particular subject matter and are always willing to share it? You might find it hard to believe that you're an influencer. An idea that is happily shared with others tends to be persuasive and influence others to either take actions or decisions on it or share with others.

If you're comfortable with being vulnerable, that is, unveiling your life activities to people who care to know, you may want to consider influencing others. Remember, you'll be talking about yourself and your family. This does not also exclude your daily routine or activities. That being said, the process - just like success - comes with its hurdles that you'll have to deal with. You can make it happen. Become a global influencer to expand your reach.

Final thoughts

Irrespective of who you are - a daughter, sister, mother, or friend - you're a source of influence to others. We influence our parents when we are growing up. We influence our co-workers at the office by the things we do. We influence our children when raising them. You have been working all your life preparing for this.

Now, all you have to do is dig down deep, find what that mission is that has been bubbling up inside you, and turn lose those beautiful skills you've been nurturing all your life. Consider the circle of friends following you who are influenced by your posts and thus are swift to pass their comments.

Connect with Jana: https://taplink.cc/bestholisticlife

"Heal from Within is incredibly comprehensive. It's the only book about health and wellness you will ever need. "

"A revolutionary, step-by-step guide to physical, emotional and spiritual healing"

A Guidebook to Intuitive Wellness

HEAL FROM WITHIN

KATIE BEECHER, LPC

Internationally Recognized Medical Intuitive

- Root cause healing
- Trauma healing
- Psychic/intuitive development
- Self-love and authenticity
- Spiritual growth

and so much more

MAGIC IS THE NEW REAL

BY LON ART

Magic.

Who does not love the idea of changing what is into what could be... of infinite possibilities, of mystery and mysticism, enchanted forests, powerful dragons, and great wizards and sorcerers? We all have, at one time or another, allowed ourselves to be carried away by the tales and stories of magical beings that had seemingly unprecedented powers to alter their reality in the blink of an eye, the wave of a wand, and the casting of a spell.

Why are we so fascinated with magic? After all, we all know that magic isn't real... don't we?

To understand our deep fascination with magic, we must first look at the mere definition of the word. According to Merriam-Webster's dictionary, magic can be described as:

"an extraordinary power or influence seemingly from a supernatural source."

This suggests that the ability to perform magic is "more than ordinary" and only for those that possess powers that are "beyond natural". Of course, these descriptions depend on our definition of "ordinary" and "natural" as well as those subject to the current paradigm. Our deep fascination also reveals our (often unconscious) desire to alter our existing reality, to change what we have into what we want, and to become a larger expression of who we currently are. Magic allows us to believe that the impossible is possible and that the unimaginable could happen.

So, perhaps what we consider to be magic is simply that which we cannot explain within the parameters of our existing belief system. Often what we believe to be real is what we believe to be true and what our rational mind can explain. Of course, many things that once were considered unexplainable and even magical have found themselves over time to be explored, analyzed, understood, and described through an ever-evolving science. Fire, rainbows, sunsets and rises, magnetics, flight, and many healing modalities are all examples of this. They all, at one time, evolved from a mystery into a fundamental part of how we understand our world and our reality. Once they were embraced by science, they became part of our existing paradigm.

And then, there are the many things we all clearly experience in one form or another in our lives that we consider being very real but cannot explain in rational or scientific terms. Amazing, yet unexplainable, things happen all the time. Sometimes they seem magical and mysterious, but often, they are things we are used to, things we take for granted and have accepted as part of our reality without realizing that they are sourced from something beyond the world of 3D and linearity—making them in fact, magical.

Love is a big one. Our desire to feel loved and love someone or something is one of the most powerful driving forces behind our evolution, our actions, our goals, our visions, and our dreams. Although we can clearly have an experience of love, we cannot really explain what it is, how it happens, or where it is inside ourselves. This makes love magical. Our relationship with a higher or divine power is another large expression of our (unconscious) belief in magic, as evidenced by the huge variety of religions all over the world and the sheer number of humans who believe in some sort of higher power or expression of the Divine. Soul, connection, and spontaneous remission are other examples of things that transcend the 3D world as well—real for many of us, yet impossible to describe or prove in a way that fully explains the joy, comfort, guidance, hope, faith, fulfillment, and motivation they can bring us.

They all fall in the realm of magic and mystery.

Now that quantum technology allows us to go beyond the boundaries of our three-dimensional world and into the realm of multidimensionality, we come to realize that nothing is actually solid and that, in fact, everything is energy. Not only are you made of energy, so is your body, the stuff around you, and even your thoughts, your words, and your beliefs. It is all energy. And, all energy is connected in a vast and infinite field that we all are part of, as much as it is part of us, and that we are in constant interaction with. Your energy, made up of the thoughts you think and the emotions you feel, is interacting with the larger field around you, causing the energy in that field to respond to you. This field is going to arrange the energy around you to match your energy, and that will be reflected in what and who shows up in your life. Now, isn't that pure magic? That you attract the circumstances and people to you based on your energy, in other words, with your thoughts, feelings, and beliefs?

Magic is the new real. By becoming aware of our thoughts, our feelings, and our beliefs, we can become conscious co-creators of our reality and our lives. This makes us the Modern Merlins, the magicians of our time.

Connect with Lon: https://modernmerlinmagic.com/

7-WAYS TO GET MORE CLIENTS FOR YOUR FITNESS BUSINESS

BY JAMES PATRICK

There are few things more stressful than needing new clients to find you. The act of generating leads is perhaps the single most important element of a business. Without a consistent method of generating new leads, you as the entrepreneur cannot make any sales and without any sales, there is no longer a business. To make matters more frustrating for entrepreneurs, many fall short of their lead-generating efforts by relying too heavily on tactics that don't actually produce work. This reactive marketing efforts include spending too much time on social media, building out an expensive website, or writing a blog hoping people will find you and your business organically. Spoiler alert, hoping is not an effective marketing strategy.

Another mistake that many entrepreneurs make is to rely exclusively on a single source for generating leads and when that source changes or dries us, so too does their business.

In efforts to diversify your lead generating efforts, or to simply inspire you with new means of attracting new clients into your ecosystem, what follows are seven ways fitness entrepreneurs, like you, can generate more leads for their business.

1. Advertising

I want to begin with paid advertising for two reasons. First, it is often the default idea that many entrepreneurs have when it comes to growing awareness and generating leads. Second, it can be stressful for those entrepreneurs who are bootstrapping and do not possess the level of finances required to yield a positive return on investment in advertising. If that is you, the false assumption is that since you cannot afford to purchase advertising, digital or traditional print, you become stuck and unable to qualify for growing your business and generating leads. It is a terrible catch 22. You need revenue to pay for advertising but you cannot pay for advertising until you create revenue. The good news is that there are plenty of other means to generate leads that do not require a significant investment in advertising. However, if you are in a position to leverage the power of advertising, it is important to gauge the cost required to generate a new business lead and the percentage of those leads that convert into clients. This is how you as a business owner can measure the effectiveness of your ad spend.

2. Word of Mouth Referrals

This is, most likely, how you as a one-to-one business owner got your start in generating leads for your business. You were able to get your close friends, family, colleagues, and associates to start referring others to do business with you. But somewhere along the way, many stop asking for referrals, and thus the word of mouth dried up. Yet this still remains one of the most effective ways to onboard new clients as the trust and rapport have already been enhanced by the referring party. If you are looking to evolve from a one-to-one business into a one-to-many business, then word of mouth should actually be orchestrated. Brainstorm various ways you could incentivize your audience to refer others to

work with you as well as equip them with the tools and resources to make the referrals as effortless as possible. These tools could include graphics for them to post, text for them to e-mail out as well as specific instructions on how to best promote your services. The incentivization could include rewards, bonus services or even monetary compensation.

3. Affiliate Program

Going one step further, you could implement a structured affiliate (or ambassador) program where individuals become independent contractors of your business, receive compensation for referrals, or are offered discounts in exchange for their services in promoting your brand.

4. Partnerships

It would behoove you as an entrepreneur to establish partnerships with other service providers in your industry. You can promote one another's services, refer businesses back and forth to one another, and offer a fuller portfolio of services to each of your clients. A branding photographer would partner with a graphic or web designer. A nutritionist could partner with a personal trainer. Alternatively, you could create digital partnerships with others in your industry to promote one another through your various channels. For example, you could interview one another via your Instagram or YouTube platforms which not only promotes you to their audience and vice versa but provides great value to the audience.

5. Lists You Own

Probably the biggest mistake entrepreneurs make is to not create a list of their own leads. You do not own your followers on social media nor are you able to always reach them. Thus, you should develop a list that you own and manage of prospective clients that you can nurture and eventually sell to. This could be an e-mail list, an SMS list, or even a traditional mailing list. The best method to grow your list is to offer something of value that your audience wants enough to join your list to receive.

6. Lists Your Rent

Did you know that you can rent lists from other businesses? To be clear, you do not receive the actual list, but you are able to pay a business to e-mail their list about your products and services. The cost will vary based upon the business selling and the size of the list, but for a well-targeted list, it can be a productive method to grow your own business leads.

7. Earned Media

Earned media is one of the fastest and most effective ways to generate new leads. This can include magazine features, podcast or television spots as well as digital features. When you get featured by a media outlet that your target demographic consumes, it provides you the opportunity to amplify your authority, establish your brand and generate new leads to enter your marketing ecosystem. Connect with James: https://jamespatrick.com/coaching/

THE 4 TYPES OF STORIES TO BOOST SOCIAL MEDIA ENGAGEMENT

BY MARIAH MACINNES

I forgot the power of storytelling on social media when I started my business. I was too busy delivering the educational content.

"The 4 things you need in a content marketing strategy".

Don't get me wrong, this is valuable content. It allows people to take this information and implement it straight away. But, maybe they don't remember what I told them? Maybe they read the post, though it was interesting, and moved on with their life without taking action?

So, when it came to March 2021 and I was lying in a hospital bed, after the removal of two tumors, I felt called to grab my phone and talk about my struggles on Instagram stories. I started to share what I was doing in the hospital, how I was feeling, and what it taught me about business.

I was sharing my story.

When I got out of the hospital and it was time to start back in my business, back to creating content, I knew I had to talk more about storytelling because after I started sharing my story, it sparked conversations. Those conversations led to more clients (in the space of 2 months I worked with 5 new long-term clients). It grew my business. Talking about health?! Not even related to my business! After that, I started to gain knowledge. A client of mine who was a public speaking coach shared with me different types of stories.

Now I am here to take you through those and add how you can apply them to your social media and content creation.

The 4 types of stories you can tell on social media!

These stories used to describe different scenarios, pain points, and lessons learned - is a powerful strategy for your social media marketing. The 4 types include:

1. Your story

Of course, this one is a no-brainer. Your own story. Your personal experiences. If you are talking about your latest offering online, how did you birth this offering? What was the story around it? Or maybe you are creating some educational content, how did you apply or learn this in your own business. Your story can also be used just for entertainment, to engage your audience.

2. A story someone has told you

The stories of others are also so powerful within the social media space. You can write or create videos sharing the experiences of others to connect to a message you are trying to convey. These stories could also be the stories of those you helped!

3. Stories in the public domain

These are the stories we all know. The famous stories. The stories we can relate back to our story or the message we want to deliver. These could be stories from those in our industry or any story we can connect to.

4. Hypothetical story

The made-up story. The one where we can use your audience as the "hero", the main lead. To take them on a journey. To get them to visualize themselves in the ideal scenario (or not so ideal scenario).

How can you use stories on social media?

Depending on the channel you are using, will depend on the type of content you create. Whether it is long written pieces, short written pieces, or videos (short or long-form).

What matters is how you blend the art of storytelling into the pieces of content you create. Maybe you write an article on LinkedIn talking about how you started in business and what lessons you learned along the way (as a "get to know your piece").

Maybe you create a sales-type Instagram caption using a hypothetical story, placing your audience in the shoes of someone who is victorious in their problem after joining your offering.

With your social media content, it is about taking the content you create now and looking at how you can start adding more storytelling. How you can blend this in to take your audience on a journey from beginning, middle, and end. Whether it is a sales-type piece of content, an educational piece or you sharing a lesson to convey a message.

How can you use stories in content marketing?

You can create blogs utilizing the different types of stories, YouTube content, and podcasts. Whatever it is. Whenever you are creating a piece of content, a story can be used to formulate a really entertaining piece.

A piece that can be remembered. Much research on storytelling shows that "stories can be up to 22 times more memorable than just the facts". It doesn't mean your whole content piece needs to be a story, but how can you weave little gold nuggets into your content by delivering a memorable story?

What is next?

If you are at the beginning of your journey in business or having influence, this is a journey I am taking you on.

Here is an exercise for you to take with you.

Exercise - Write down a story for each of the 4 types listed above, doesn't have to be perfect, this is just to get you started. Once you are ready to action these stories, download my FREE guide to storytelling and start getting ready to share online!

Storytelling helped me connect with my audience, it helped me build my business and now I am here to show you how it can help you too!

Connect with Mariah: https://www.contentqueenmariah.com/instagram/

Story Telling Guide

TIPS AND TRICKS FOR GETTING STARTED WITH CANVA

BY COREY WALKER

Making decisions in alignment with our soul and defining success on our own terms.

If you're like most small business owners, you're always looking for ways to save time and streamline your operations. That's why Canva is such a popular tool – it allows you to create high-quality graphics without spending hours in Photoshop or Illustrator. In this post, I'll share some tips and tricks for getting the most out of Canva. Whether you're just starting out or you've been using Canva for a while, there's sure to be something here that will help you take your designs to the next level!

Getting Started

Since most of what I design now is for social media, I'll be focusing on that in this article. To get started, go to Canva.com and create an account. They have free accounts that let you design at no charge, but they charge you for some graphics individually. The Pro account is $12.95 a month and includes all stock photography, a magic resizing tool, the ability to upload your brand's fonts, create folders, and share designs with other team members. I highly recommend the Pro account if you create graphics regularly.

Creating a New Design

The beauty of Canva is that it's very user-friendly. If you would like to create an Instagram post, simply go to the top of the page and select "Instagram Post." Canva then provides a perfect 1080x1080 pixel square to begin. If you need some inspiration to get started, use one of their templates, but tweak it with your colors, fonts, and imagery. I normally discourage clients from using the template as-is because you want your brand to be reflected in your posts. The other option is to begin designing on your own, pulling in photos or other graphics. You can use the Upload tool to upload your own photos. Once uploaded, simply drag the photo over to your blank canvas. You can also choose one of Canva's stock photos from the Photos area if you don't have any of your own. Canva has a robust photo offering, and you can search for different types of photos or backgrounds.

Adding Text

Once you have your main background set, you may want to add text. To add text, tap Text on the left-hand navigation bar. If you have a brand kit set up with a specific font, it will default to that. Otherwise, it will have a basic font to choose from that you can change. For basic text, tap on either the Headline, Subheading, or Body Text to bring it onto your canvas. There are also fun font combinations underneath that if you are looking for something more unique.

Going Beyond the Basics

If you're ready to level up your design, get to know the Elements area. This is where you can add shapes, or a frame where you can add a photo. You can also add a number of other elements like lines, stickers, graphics, videos, audio, tables, and more. I highly encourage you to play around with these to see how you can jazz up your designs. There are so many possibilities!

Saving and Downloading

Your design is saving along the way periodically, which is nice in the instance that your computer decides to quit on you! To easily find your design again, you'll want to go to the top blue bar of the screen and give the image a name. Once saved, you can download the image to your computer to use later. Canva has many file types to choose from. For a social media graphic, you'll want to choose a png file. If you inserted any video, you'll want to download the image as an mp4. Once downloaded, upload the image to your favorite social media platform. Bonus tip: if you have the Pro account, you can use the Resize tool to resize the image for a different platform. For instance, if I create an image from Instagram that I also want to use on Twitter, I can tell Canva to resize it for Twitter, and it will make a copy and resize it. It's not always perfect, so you may need to tweak it a little bit, but it's much easier than starting from scratch. That's all there is to it! Canva has been a lifesaver for me. I used InDesign, PhotoShop, and Illustrator for years, and now I hardly ever open those programs. It's a one-stop-shop, not only for social media, but for flyers, presentations, brochures, and even ebooks! I encourage you to give it a try!

Connect with Corey: www.TheMarketingSpecialist.com

Instagram checklist

BUSY IS A CHOICE

BY JEFF WICKERSHAM

There is an underlying current that has taken a hold of who we are as humans.

It has taken a hold of our society.

It's sneaky.

You don't know how it got here or how you adopted it yet you feel the stress of it each day.

It was a subtle shift, I'm not even sure when it happened, but the cost you are paying for it is with your life.

It's a default pattern we have learned, adopted, and now operate with.

It takes up our days, weeks, months, and years.

It's our default response when someone asks you either how you're doing or how was your day?

The answer?

Busy.

To be honest, how often do you respond with that automatic answer of 'busy'?

It's not your fault, but it's your responsibility to fix it.

Do you think we were designed to run from meeting to meeting, email to email on our workdays?

If you're a parent like I am, do you think your family time should be spent eating a meal in the car as you go from one activity to the next?

Do you think life is to be lived by ending your day exhausted, stressed, flopping on the couch with nothing left, and feeling like you got nothing accomplished?

I'll save you the suspense. You are not meant to operate that way.

We are not machines.

We cannot go, go, go and think that it will not have a negative impact on us.

The results of this never-ending go, go, go lifestyle?

Stress at all-time highs.

Obese and overweight adults at a staggering 72%.

It's time to stop the madness.

It's time to make a different choice.

Make no mistake about it, you do have a choice.

You have a choice to be busy or not.

It's what I do for a living as a peak performance coach, helping others make a choice to step into the best version of themselves.

One of the greatest decisions my wife and I ever made as parents was to take a sports season off three years ago.

It was a tough decision, but we knew in our hearts and souls that we needed to make that choice. To choose not to be 'busy' for even just a small bit of time.

Below is the letter I wrote and read to them with tears streaming down my face:

To my sons, Jackson and Carter,

Your mom and I made the decision for you to take the spring off from sports so you can focus on being a kid. This wasn't an easy decision, but I know in my heart it's the right one. I want you to laugh, run, joke, get dirty, play with your friends, have sleepovers, chase lightening bugs, dream, do whatever your mind can imagine. This time is yours to enjoy.

I realize how demanding sports can be at a young age. I want to be sure you develop a life-long love of exercise and sports as I have. Sometimes, in order to do that you need to take a break from the heat of competition. You need your body to recover and your mind to rest.

You have both had amazing years in football and basketball. I've had the privilege of coaching you both and would not trade it for the world. The sky is the limit and I believe you will achieve greatness. I am so incredibly proud of you both.

I also know that your time under our roof is limited, and I want to maximize the time I have with both of you. I want to create memories and experiences that we will remember for the rest of our lives. Let's camp in the woods, dance in the ocean, hike up mountains, eat ice cream until our bellies hurt and appreciate the moments we have together. This does not mean we will not be active; in fact, we might actually be more active, but we will do it as a family and on our own terms. Too often in life, we live on terms that are not our own. Let this be an example that you can live your life however you want to and never let anyone tell you differently. I'm so excited for the days to get longer and the sun to grow warmer! You both being born are the greatest moments of my life.

I love you.

Dad

I shared that personal letter to inspire you to take action.

To inspire you that your life is not meant to be busy.

To inspire you, if you're a parent, take time to create memories with your children as you only get 18 summers with them. Remember, you have a choice.

You have a choice to choose differently in your life.

You have the power to choose to take control of your days.

You have the power to live life to the fullest and play on your own terms.

You have the power to say no to things that aren't core to who you are.

Busy is a choice and you have the power to change it.

Live your best life!!

Connect with Jeff: https://linktr.ee/morningfire

Complimentary
20-minute coaching! →

YOU ARE UNSTOPPABLE.

HERE'S PROOF:

BY VIRGINIA OMAN LCMHC NCPT

Have you ever felt hopeless, like all life's joys were no longer reachable for you? I have. And having climbed my way back out, I am passionate about sharing my message of hope, so others don't have to feel that level of despair that I once did. Due to a progressive neurological condition, I lost all ability to walk. I lost all energy in my body and had to nap throughout the day. I lost the ability to work and participate in life. And no longer able to work, I lost my home. Knowing the condition was going to continue, I lost the most important thing on earth, hope. I found that to be the worst kind of despair one can feel. So, at the very last point, where I was going to exit out with absolutely nothing left to lose, I decided to listen to my own intuition instead of what the "professionals" had been advising. I took a long deep breath and regrouped. Using all resources inside me, I developed my own tools using the incredible mind-body connection. I designed a specific plan, and then I followed it one day at a time. No immediate results but my desire to keep living was so strong I stuck to it no matter how difficult. And THAT made all the difference. Continuity. One step at a time. No matter what.... keep following the plan. Believe. And then it all started to change. I got more energy! Encouraged, I stayed with it, and then the "unbelievable" started to happen. I am now being called a "miracle" .... "phenomenal"...as I am walking, dancing, hiking, swimming laps, and I even used my specific plan of action to be able to ride a 2-wheel bicycle again which is something everyone including my doctors said would be "impossible." I am working and living a full life with more joy and energy than ever before. And I'm here to tell you, I am not a miracle. I am merely proof that if you know how to harness what is already inside you, you CAN do anything you set your mind to. If you can vividly see it, want it more than anything else...and take daily action on it...you can get there. You need a plan. I devote my life now to sharing the specific plan and focus areas I used so anyone can have life-changing results. Regardless of ANYTHING that makes them stuck in despair. These specific focus areas I used are all 100% holistic and 100% free. How great is THAT! No matter what you feel is holding you back from the joy and fulfillment that is your inherent birthright, there IS a way beyond. Each of us is born with a unique spark of energy and life that is meant to flourish during this lifetime. Just like each flower comes from a seed and inside that seed is the spark of life to grow and grow and become that unique beautiful flower. You are too. Don't let your life pass you by without bringing that unique life into the world and filling you with the joy you deserve. It is right here waiting for you. Think it's impossible? Nothing, and I mean NOTHING could be farther from the truth.

Connect with Virginia: https://virginiaoman.com/

Secrets to the Powerful Mind Body Connection

EYE SEE A HEALTHIER LIFE IN YOUR FUTURE

BY DR. DEE

When it comes to your health we all know how important it is to keep your eyes on the prize. It's not just about having a vision for the life you want, it's about supporting your whole body's needs. One of the organs that often gets overlooked more than any others in our eyes! Let's be honest, at the end of the day, we don't realize just how important something is or how often we use it until there is something wrong with it. Unfortunately, when it comes to our eye health in most cases it is not like a light switch that flicks on and off. In most cases, our eye health slowly declines and as such, we fail to notice just how bad things are until they reach dangerous levels. One of the biggest hurdles we face with eye health is blood flow. Blood flow is one of the most important things for our whole body. Nutrients and toxin elimination are essential for supporting health throughout the body.

Circulation is everything! Most people don't realize just how little circulation actually makes it to the eyes. In spite of the fact that the eyeball is fluid encased at all sides and kept safe and lubricated. Our eyes are exposed almost constantly with little to no blood flow connection. The one main point of blood flow stems from the optical root. Unfortunately, the root doesn't provide enough circulation for the eyes over an extended period of time.

Another downside to this limited connection of circulation the eyes are often one of the first parts of the body to suffer. Hypertension can be disastrous for the entire body. However, the first place it hits, as well as the area that hit the hardest, is the eyes. The excess strain on your blood pressure causes pressure to build up in your eyes as well as your head. Remember, blood flow matters, it not only removes toxins to be eliminated, but it also directs vitamins, minerals, and nutrients where they need to be.

While there are tons of things you can do to help support your eye health. The first thing I would suggest is to make the swap to an anti-inflammatory diet. Doing so helps your whole body and of course your eye health. There are a variety of vitamins and minerals that help support and improve your eye health. The best vitamins to support your eye health are vitamins C, E, B1 (thiamine), and Omega-3 fatty acids. Whereas the minerals that are essential for eye health are zinc, copper, lutein, and zeaxanthum.

While there are a number of ways you can get these vitamins and minerals into your daily routine. My personal favorite way to do just that is through nutrition. The best foods to reach for are fish, nuts, legumes, seeds, citrus fruits, leafy green vegetables, carrots, sweet potatoes, eggs, lean beef, and of course water! Don't underestimate the importance of water. Our bodies are made up of mostly water and it is important to keep the status quo.

Another key ingredient to help love your eyes is reducing stress! Stress is at the root of all illnesses. While stress has a way of working its way into every facet of our lives. It can have devastating effects on more than just our bodies. Stress breaks our bodies down slowly. As such, just like our eye health, when something slowly degrades over a long period of time we tend not to notice until it is too late. That's why it's imperative to do as much preventative work as possible. It's important to spot the signs early and do everything you can to support your health.

When it comes to spotting the signs of degrading eye health there are a few things to keep an eye out for blurred vision, eye strain, pressure headaches, dry eyes, itchiness, and more. It's important to have your doctor check your eyes regularly at least once a year. Your eyes are the lens you use to envision your life and complete daily tasks. They

Meet Dr. Dee

are the windows to more than just your soul. So make sure you treat them right and detox regularly and often. Keeping your body free of toxins and free radicals is necessary to maintain a healthy life and a healthy mind. There are tons of foods you can add to your regular diet to help your body with its critical detoxifying processes. If you are looking for a safe and all-natural way to detox your body at home be sure to check out my Balancing Abundance Program. Because detoxing is so important and realistically everyone should be doing it on at least a seasonal basis I have taken the time to put together a program to help you do just that. Here's the thing, I know working with me one-on-one can seem diffi-cult to get into (due to limited space) and I wanted to be able to give everyone an additional solution that has no limits. You deserve to be happy, healthy, and success-ful at everything you do so here are some recipes to help

set you up for success!

Need A Hand?

A happy and healthy life is closer than you may think. We all have to deal with our health daily, and when we don't feel our best, it shows. If you are tired of just making it through your day, you NEED to start investing in your health today! You are not alone on this journey. If you ever need any help, I am always here to do just that. Even if it is something as small as acting as a sounding board, do you have any questions or concerns I can help you with? Feel free to contact me directly at DrDeeandMe@ gmail.com, or you can even book a one-on-one call with me. Be sure to subscribe to gain access to tons of free goodies and check back daily for more great recipes and information!

Connect with Dr. Dee: https://askdrdee.taplink.ws

Free Offer

Meet Taylor

BACK OFF THE BIOHACKING AND GET BACK TO THE BASICS

BY TAYLOR SAPPINGTON

I know, advice that goes against everything we are being told to do in this day and age.

All you have to do is flip on the TV, pull up Facebook, or hop on Instagram to get a dose of what is being served up to better your body.

We have gadgets, lotions, pills, and potions that promise to take care of all your ails with a few uses or a few bottles.

And while I love that human ingenuity has made its way to the front of the line I often question what it's stepped on to get there.

With so many infected with **shiny new object syndrome** many have forgotten or do not know where to begin when it comes to the basics of the body.

We have women who don't understand the parameters of their cycle or how to track it and men that have little insight on how detrimental that plastic bottle actually is to their sex hormone balance.

Naturally, this question is bound to come next in the conversation...

Are you suggesting I pause on the purchase of the latest and greatest invention to hit the market, the invention that promises to finally get me to the next best version of myself Taylor?

Yes, I am indeed.

I'm going to take it a step further and ask you to reflect on the idea that the best version of you already exists.

Imagine the possibility that awaits if you chose to turn down the dial on the noise of your outer environment and tune into the frequency of your body.

What would that frequency sound like?

How would that frequency feel as it's pulsing through your veins?

What would this frequency teach and tell you when you gave it your undivided attention?

We seek a hack for almost every habit in our life.

A hack to wake up earlier

A hack to sleep deeper and more restfully

A hack for great amounts of sustained energy

A hack to get us tapped into our emotions and subconscious quicker

A hack to quiet or completely eliminate the symptoms our body uses as a means of communicating to get our attention.

If we are of the earth and the Mother Nature is known to not rush a thing would that not also apply to us?

What we are being asked to better understand is that one cannot rush their healing.

In fact, I would argue a critical component to whole-body healing is knowing what our foundational needs look like and taking the appropriate steps in service and support of our body.

Do we actually think any of these hacks effectively work if the basic needs of the body are not being met?

I am inviting you to take a deeper look at the concept that healing doesn't actually begin until you come to better understand all bodies that are seeking your support.

The mental body

The emotional body

The spiritual body

... and, yes, the physical body.

This means co-creating a relationship that allows for the intimacy and vulnerability needed to take a peek into our best and brightest beliefs while also courageously giving ourselves permission to allow for the illumination of our darkest and deepest nooks and crannies of need.

Growth comes from becoming aware of, acknowledging, and taking action on those deep dark nooks and crannies of need.

I am going to throw another radical concept for contemplation at you, perhaps the invitation is simply to prioritize the relationship we as human beings are meant to have with the basic elements needed to function such as clean food and water, stable shelter, and a deep connection with our community as opposed to perpetually seeking out a new invention as a means of intervention to make up for what's missing.

You can't build a house from the top down placing the roof on first and expect a stable structure.

That same principle applies to building back and up to one's health.

It all starts at ground level with careful intention and effort put towards creating a solid foundation.

So, how does one go about starting the journey back home to their body?

It's simple...

Let the sun kiss your skin for 15 to 30 minutes a day

Place your hands AND feet in the dirt; yes, GET DIRTY, it's good for your health.

Drink, bathe, and cook using clean water; think filtered or spring sourced.

Step outside and remind yourself what it's like to connect with your breath while filling your lungs full of fresh ozone rich air

Let mother earth hold you.

Some of life's best medicine is free. Lay on the ground and look up at the sky to tap into the great remembering of who you are and where you came from.

The reality of it is, the best approach to biohacking the body is to back off.

Connect with Taylor:
https://linktr.ee/tayloredwellbeing

taylored wellbeing

Free Offer

4-WAYS TO HELP HIGHLY INTUITIVE KIDS

BY KIERSTEN PARSONS-HATHCOCK

Many of us want to build better habits. We want to lose weight, eat healthier, or get better sleep. When we look at our lives, we see something that could be improved.

But when we try to implement new habits, we discover the information is all over the place, like the common misnomer that it takes 21 days to build a habit. (The statistic comes frI was seven when I remember first seeing them. They were like regular people only they'd vanish at a moment's notice. Over time, I learned not to talk about the shadowy figures I saw because, every time I did, someone would tell me that I was mistaken. That nothing was there. Or worse, that I was making it up.

Eventually, they stopped coming around—or rather I stopped being open to seeing them. That is until I turned thirty-six years old.

Here's the thing: I didn't know, at the age of seven, that I was a highly intuitive child. It wasn't something people talked about in my small Ohio town. Looking back, I wish I'd known more about heightened sensory perception. Learning to trust your gut at a young age helps prepare you to use intuition as a roadmap for life.

Now, as a 48-year-old intuitive medium with two kids of my own, I fully understand how important it is to help children learn the value of their intuition. Over the past ten years, I've mentored many kids and young adults, and have discovered a few practices that best help them learn to trust themselves.

Here are four ways you can help your highly intuitive child:

1. BELIEVE THEM. I know first-hand how hard it is to believe in things you can't explain. As a parent, you're responsible for making sure your children value truth over lies. It can be quite triggering to hear your little one talk about things you can't see for yourself. Most highly intuitive children will share details that are very specific. Their descriptions are typically detailed and wise beyond their years, and in some cases, children will talk about past lives they remember. Support them as best you can and seek out mentors and specialists as you see fit. Trust your own intuition as you navigate parenting a highly intuitive child.

2. ENCOURAGE THEM TO SET BOUNDARIES. In order to take control of what can feel out of control and scary at times, children need to set boundaries. For example, ask kids to make rules for what they'll allow in and around them. I ask each child that I mentor to write up rules that can be posted in their home, room, etc. (Rule number 1: Only energies that are good for me are allowed in my home. Rule number 2: I do not allow energies to wake me up while I'm sleeping. And so on.) When children (and adults) realize they are truly in charge, their whole world changes for the better.

3. TEACH THEM ABOUT PROTECTING THEIR ENERGY IN CROWDS. Many highly intuitive kids are easily overwhelmed in crowds and are highly sensitive to energy in general. One technique I've used with younger kids is to teach them to envision a white ball of light wrapping around them. They can also envision donning a cape of light before they walk into school. Because the intention is energy, the cape or bubble will help protect them from absorbing other people's energy. According to scientific research, the human body consists of energy vibrating at specific rates. This vibrational energy produces a magnetic field around the body known as the bio-energetic field or aura. The aura surrounds about 4 feet to 5 feet of an area around the human body. This means, when a child walks down a hallway at school or sits close to friends in a classroom, their energy fields will mesh.

Kiersten Parsons Hathcock

4. HELP THEM IDENTIFY PHYSICAL SIGNS OF INTUITION. Intuition is known for being very subtle at times. This is why it's important to also teach highly intuitive kids how to recognize bodily signs and feelings. For example, the gut-punch feeling is a common sign indicating a warning. Tightness in the chest or stomach aches can also indicate unease. Chills that run up and down the body are another common intuition indicator that typically means there's truth to what is happening in the moment.

Teaching highly intuitive kids to value their intuition helps them learn to navigate the world, both as kids and later on as adults. Instead of feeling fear, uncertainty, and shame related to their intuitive skills, they can learn to feel good about their inner knowing and use it to light their way.

Author, Little Voices: How Kids in Spirit Helped a Reluctant Medium Escape and Heal from Abuse
Connect with Kiersten: https://taplink.cc/kierstenhathcockany days

Free Intuition Guide

How to

BECOME THE NEXT
GLOBAL INFLUENCER!

Join Jana on this
Four Part Video Series to:

- Learn The Power of your STORY
- Develop Your Unique Branding
- Build A Media Kit That Opens Doors
- Use Blogging To Educate and
  Lead To Your Programs

Learn more and sign up for this LIMITED TIME OFFER. Instead of ~~$997~~ only **$97**

Jana Short
FIRE. HOPE. COURAGE

LEARN MORE OR SIGN UP!

HOW TO TREAT PCOS NATURALLY

BY DR. LULU SHIMEK

DR. LULU

Igniting
Cellular
Freedom™

Discover how to heal
your PCOS naturally

WHAT IS PCOS?

Polycystic Ovarian Syndrome (PCOS) is the most common complex endocrine dysfunction in women of reproductive age with hormonal irregularities. Originally it was classified as a hormonal disorder, but as more was learned about PCOS and its origins the presence of polycystic ovaries is just one of its manifestations. The root cause of the imbalance is multi-faceted, but PCOS is primarily a metabolic condition associated with insulin resistance and the overproduction of androgens.

WHAT ARE THE CAUSES OF PCOS?

The underlying cause of PCOS is often misunderstood. The classic cause of PCOS results in anovulation when the ovaries fail to release an egg during the menstrual cycle due to elevated levels of estrogen, LH (luteinizing hormone), and testosterone (androgens). This leads to decreased levels of progesterone and FSH (follicle-stimulating hormone) causing continued follicular growth without follicular maturity or chronic anovulation. Chronic anovulation is also a common cause of infertility. When under stress, the adrenal system also affects PCOS by elevating DHEA levels and in turn increasing androgen levels. There have been several studies that demonstrate a genetic component (autosomal dominant) with symptoms of hyperinsulinemia, alopecia, anovulation, polycystic ovaries, and hyperandrogenism. These genetic factors can be turned on or off by epigenetic factors such as stress, inflammation, poor nutrition, elevated insulin levels, sedentary lifestyle, birth control, and use of bio-identical hormone replacement therapy (BHRT).

HOW IS PCOS DIAGNOSED?

Making a diagnosis of PCOS can be complicated because of the combination of overlapping symptoms with other hormonal disorders, and not all root causes of PCOS are the same. It's important to have blood tests completed and properly evaluated for hormone imbalances and to also screen for insulin resistance. An ultrasound of the ovaries is the last step in diagnosis but about 20% of women with PCOS do not have polycystic ovaries so it's also important to rule out endometriosis.

WHAT ARE THE COMMON SYMPTOMS OF PCOS?

The symptoms of PCOS are varied so it's important to check in with your naturopathic doctor or health care practitioner for a proper diagnosis. These are some of the most common symptoms seen in patients with PCOS.

Absent or missed periods	Hair loss
Irregular bleeding	Hair growth on the face or body
Insulin resistance	Weight gain and obesity
Infertility	Extreme hunger or thirst
Dark ring around the neck	Inflammation
Adult acne	Fatigue

Take my PCOS quiz to see if your symptoms suggest PCOS.

https://www.tryinteract.com/share/quiz/6246226011a9d1001801d5eb

NATURAL SOLUTIONS FOR PCOS

When it comes to treating PCOS, it's all about my proven four system approach: nutrition, cycle balancing, stress management, and nutraceuticals.

NUTRITION:

With insulin-resistant PCOS being the most common type it's imperative to examine and change the nutritional plan and diet. It's important to focus on foods that are going to optimize your hormonal health, reduce inflammation, balance blood sugar, and are loaded with healthy fats.

BALANCING YOUR CYCLE:

One of the main symptoms of PCOS is irregular bleeding and missed cycles so proper cycle tracking and hormonal support is fundamental for this stage of the healing. This phase starts by opening the detoxification process of the liver to assist the body to metabolize and dispose of toxins. When the body is in a toxic state and not eliminating properly, the toxins build up and cause hormonal imbalance. A genetic test including the MTHFR gene can help determine toxicity levels and elimination functions.

STRESS MANAGEMENT:

We live in a stressful and toxic world with emotional, physical, and chemical stressors impacting the hormones. To fully address the inflammatory nature of PCOS, stress management techniques need to be used daily to re-establish balance within the parasympathetic nervous system, resting and digesting. As you probably know, our body responds to stress in many ways. It could be headaches, PMS, weight gain, fatigue, insomnia, libido, or chronic pain. To address the inflammatory nature of PCOS, mindful breathing techniques, daily movement, and meditation practices will reset the stress pathway and hormones.

NUTRACEUTICALS:

The focus of supplement and botanical medicine in healing PCOS is to modulate hormones and hormonal signaling to the ovaries, balance menstrual irregularities, reduce inflammation, manage stress, and if needed promote fertility optimization.

Here are a few of the nutraceuticals I have seen to be most effective with PCOS cases. In research studies, inositol has been shown to enhance ovarian function as well as reduce hyperandrogenism. Omega 3 fatty acids are helpful in hormone metabolism and reducing serum triglycerides, especially in diabetics. For balancing blood sugar and reducing lipids, the herb Gymnema acts as a trophorestorative for the beta cells of the pancreas in producing more insulin and pancreatic enzymes. Chaste berry or Vitex can be useful for low progesterone levels as well as infertility associated with a poor functioning corpus luteum.

WE ARE NOT ALL CREATED EQUAL

An important aspect of PCOS is that not all women have the same symptoms, hormonal imbalance, nutritional needs, and stress. Work with your naturopathic doctor to help discern if you have PCOS, the root cause, and the steps needed to bring your body back to optimal wellness.

Need more help? Get your copy of Dr. LuLu's Guide - Natural Treatments for PCOS. https://chipper-crafter-6073.ck.page/3294a5e4f4

Ready to learn more about how to care for your PCOS, what type of PCOS you have, how sugar affects PCOS and more natural therapies? Join Dr. LuLu's 4-week PCOS group healing course: Healing Your PCOS Naturally. https://doclulu.com/healing-your-pcos-naturally

Connect with Dr. LuLu: https://taplink.at/en/profile/8993130/pages/

Healing Using Medical and Spiritual Intuition

BY KATIE BEECHER

Root Cause Healing Using Medical and Spiritual Intuition

Before moving into the content of this article, it is important to provide a definition of two important terms: root cause healing and medical intuition. Root cause healing means detecting and addressing all the possible physical, emotional, and spiritual elements that impact health. Ideally, this is how you would expect and hope that all practitioners approach wellness, but sadly, this is not the case. Root cause healing isn't about just treating symptoms. It is about permanent healing and prevention.

Medical intuition is when an individual uses intuitive information to detect and address physical health concerns. As both a medical intuitive and a Licensed Professional counselor, I am in a unique position to address the physical, emotional, and spiritual issues of my clients through a clinical and more spiritual lens. Using only a name and age, before ever seeing a photo or talking with my client in person or in any other manner, my guides and I create a highly accurate, detailed, individualized report and intuitive soul painting. I send this to my clients before we meet. During the meeting, we discuss the report along with any other issues that are important to the client. My guides offer insight, guidance, tools, and a plan going forward. I also work with numerous health professionals for confirmation, diagnosis, and medical treatment since it is illegal and unethical for anyone who isn't a licensed medical professional to present diagnoses or make healing claims. The goal of my work with people is to identify and address all possible root causes and strengths that contribute to the quality of life, healthy relationships, healing trauma, self-esteem, finding their life purpose, and physical, emotional, and spiritual health. I also teach people how to connect to intuition and develop their intuitive and psychic gifts. Every

session is unique, and people are often surprised to learn that the issue they contacted me about is related to other areas of the body and issues in their life they may have long forgotten.

If you just want to know what kind of herbs or supplements to take or what foods to eat or avoid, I would not be a good match. While I can give you that information, the work I do and the work I help YOU do goes much deeper. I will challenge you to work on loving yourself, trusting your intuition, listening to your body, reducing stress and anxiety, allowing yourself to feel emotions you may be avoiding, and building your autonomy and abilities to self-advocate. I provide support and encouragement as you take steps toward ending unhappy relationships, starting a new career or business, setting healthy boundaries, and using your psychic and intuitive gifts. I will help you see how trauma you have survived and may still need to process, relates to your physical and emotional symptoms. I will help you ground and live in the present, rather than remaining stuck in the past or always dreaming about the future. I believe in individualized healing and wellness, not one size fits all protocols.

I believe that emotional challenges and physical symptoms are signals from spirit and our intuition that we need to live more authentically. This may include making changes like improved self-care, creating a stronger relationship with spirit and intuition, using our voice, leaving people and jobs that no longer serve us, and setting healthy boundaries in dysfunctional relationships. If we listen when we are first nudged, such as when we start to feel tired, have difficulty sleeping, have minor aches and pains, feel unorganized or overwhelmed, or contract a minor illness like a cold, it can be easier to resolve the necessary issues. However, when we continue to ignore concerns in our lives, our bodies may be shocked into change and awareness due to a significant illness or injury, the end of a relationship, a major accident, or losing a job or a significant amount of money.

My personal healing journey began when I sought help for a serious eating disorder and depression when I was a teenager. I am fortunate to have been healed for over 30 years and I will always be grateful for the experience, even the most difficult parts. If it were not for the pain, I would not have been motivated to change and learn to work with my spiritual gifts. Recovery helped me to find self-love, connect to intuition, disconnect from dysfunctional, toxic people, and become a therapist. I would not have found my mission, my life purpose, or have written my book, Heal from Within: A Guidebook to Intuitive Wellness. In my first book, I am honored to help teach readers how to trust their own intuition, develop their spiritual gifts, and enhance their life and health from a root cause perspective, using information from my guides, Jungian psychology, and my own individualized techniques that I have created.

Want to learn more about the possible root causes and spiritual lessons of your own symptoms and experiences and take steps toward healing? Here are some suggestions, which are discussed in detail in my book. I prefer to do this in writing so that it gets the ideas and feelings out of my head and body. It also helps me to create a visual roadmap that I can refer to and change over time. My book includes further quizzes, checklists, templates, charts, writing prompts, and other specific exercises to guide you.

1. Identify one issue you would like to work on. You may have many but start with only one so that you can give it your full attention and feel less overwhelmed.

2. Make an honest list of how that issue is impacting you, your physical, emotional, and spiritual self, your loved ones, your career, etc. List positive and detrimental effects. As I stated above, it is important to approach things holistically from all perspectives. We have enough negativity in our lives, often coming from our own guilt, perfectionism, false beliefs, fear, low self-esteem, or body dysmorphia.

3. Ask yourself what was going on in your life when the event occurred, or symptoms started. Where were you living? What stressors did you have? Any loss or changes? What were your relationships like? Did you begin or stop taking any medications or supplements? What was your spiritual life like? Any other physical or emotional symptoms? Had you traveled? Everything is potentially important.

4. Did you have any signals or intuitive inklings regarding the issue before it started or as it was beginning? How many of those did you pay attention to or ignore?

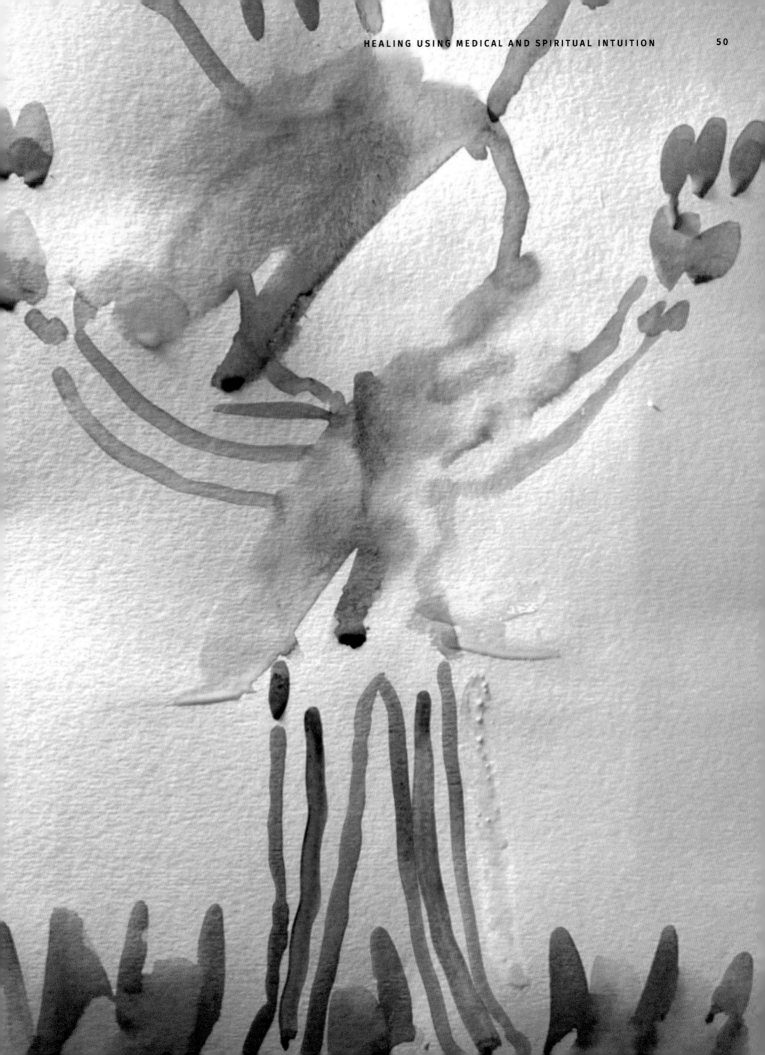

5. Do your issues seem to follow a pattern? Do they all seem to be centered around a certain area of your body, physically, emotionally, or spiritually? My book teaches you about chakras (energy centers in the body) and how to identify where your issues fit. For instance, I often discover that people who have issues with their reproductive systems like endometriosis, polycystic ovarian syndrome or infertility, or issues with their hips and lower back, have been sexually abused or assaulted or have been exposed to people who do not respect women or who are afraid of female energy and power. This all relates to the second chakra. People with thyroid issues may have difficulty connecting with feelings and expressing themselves. This relates to the fifth chakra in the throat.

6. Write down anything that comes to mind that might be interfering with healing or seeking help. Even something that seems insignificant might be important. You might even be afraid to heal because it means positive changes that you don't think you are ready for.

7. Make a list of possible actions you can take toward change and healing. This includes adjusting your mindset and being more authentic.

8. Pick just ONE thing from the list above, something not too complicated or time-consuming, and DO IT. It's okay if it takes several tries or if you temporarily give up. Go back to it and make a commitment to do it for yourself. Once you do, you will wonder what you were so afraid of and why you had put it off for so long. Allow yourself to enjoy your accomplishment and give yourself credit. Don't immediately jump to the next thing you feel you need to do or berate yourself for not doing it "good enough" or sooner.

9. Pick something else from your list and repeat step 8.

Reminder: You don't need to be a medical intuitive to use medical intuition for healing and growth. It isn't magical or "woo woo", it is simply listening to the wisdom inside of yourself and from spirit, which is always available and always has your back.

Connect with Katie: https://linktr.ee/kbeecher

$20 off a Reading use Code:
20$OFF

A Guidebook to
Intuitive Wellness

HEAL
FROM
WITHIN

KATIE BEECHER, LPC
Internationally Recognized Medical Intuitive

5 – NAVY SEAL SECRETS OF LIFE TRANSITIONS

BY WILLIAM BRANUM

Meet William

Typically you would not think about Navy SEALs, Money Management, and life transitions in the same thought, but hear me out, I think there's a lesson here.

I was interviewed recently on the Naked Wealth podcast, by Jennifer Aube, a certified financial planner. Most of our conversations revolved around Life Transitions.

Think about this: Have you ever gotten married? Bought a house? Lived through a global pandemic? Lost a loved one? Changed jobs? Got a divorce?

These are all Life Transitions, and in all these transitions, planning can make all the difference.

We all go through these transitions, but do we do it well? Sometimes they are easy because we planned them. Other life transitions leave us lost because we didn't see them coming or we were in denial about them happening, and it's hard to plan for the latter, but not impossible.

I have certainly been through my fair share of life transitions. Be it moving with the military, retiring from the Navy, or starting another new business. Some were easy and some were hard.

The important thing to remember is that Life Transitions happen all the time and we CAN and SHOULD be prepared for them.

In the SEAL Teams, we prepare for the transitions present in every mission we conduct. For example, we transition from our base to bad guy land. From inside an armored vehicle to walking the rest of the way to the target. From outside the target building to inside the target building.

From inside the building to our vehicles, and so on and so on...

The reason we put effort into planning each of those transitions, even though they seem simple, is because those are the times we are the most vulnerable.

Think about the transitions you go through every day, getting in your car, pulling out of a parking lot, driving through an intersection... Moving from one environment to another. You never know what or who is on the other side until you get there.

This article will help prepare you for the transitions of life. The transitions we know are coming and the ones we hope will never happen. Like I said before, on a SEAL Team mission, transitions are the times we are the most vulnerable. The same is true in life, transitions are the times we are the most vulnerable. If we are prepared for them, we set ourselves up for success.

As I transitioned from the SEAL Teams to civilian life, I made a terrible mistake.

I didn't plan for that transition.

I was in denial about getting out of the military. I mean, the military is all I have ever known. I kinda had an idea of what I might do...or want to do but was not at all ready when it happened.

From my failures and successes, I've put together 5 steps to help you get through any transition life throws at you.

5 SEAL Secrets to Life Transitions

Create a plan: This doesn't need to be a perfect plan. It does need to have the 5W's pretty well answered though.

Who is the plan for? (Me) I lost my job during the economic crash.

What are the actions that need to be taken? Figure out what I want to do next. Build a solid resume'. Take classes online to learn a new skill or certification.

Where will the actions take place? I need to move myself/my family to a new state that has the jobs I am looking for.

When will you take action? I start taking classes online now in the evenings to see if this is something I really want to do, and while I still have income.

Why are you taking this action? The company I work for is being negatively affected by the prices that inflation is causing.

Brief the plan: This is where you share your plan with your friends, family, or anyone you truce, where you answer the 5W's.

Dirt Dive: (not what it sounds like LOL!) This is probably the most critical part and one of the things that separate the BEST from the rest... This is practicing the plan before you execute the plan. Get together with the people you trust and ask "What if...". Shoot holes in the plan and figure out contingencies to all the things that could go wrong.

Execute the plan: Take the classes. Get the certifications. Find a new job. Quit the old job. Move the family. You will fail if you don't take action. Take action.

After action review: What did you do right? What went wrong? How do you incorporate what you did right in the future? How do you correct the things that went wrong?

Life transitions are scary, and we all go through them, but those who prepare, succeed. Retiring from the SEAL Teams after 26 years of service was a major life transition for me. I have gone through several more since then. These steps have reduced the stress and set me up for success every time, and I know they will help you.

If you would like to learn more on how to think like a Navy SEAL, check the link below to get 5 SEAL Secrets (Learn How to Think Like a Navy SEAL). Together we will make the world a better place, one life transition at a time.

Connect with William: https://liinks.co/william.branum

5 Secrets to Learn How to Think Like a Navy SEAL

NO TIME TO PLAN – COUNT ON THE PROS

BY LAVINA GOMES

How to find the time to plan your Virtual Events?

No time to plan? Count on the pros, so you are not alone!

Event planning takes a great toll on your time, especially when it's not your everyday task. The high stakes, high pressure, and high visibility of planning can be very stressful as you strive to meet the expectation of the event.

Let's face the reality; planning a big event isn't the same as organizing a small party for your friends or family members. Being in two places at the same time is not possible. There is a tendency of being overwhelmed along the way. You may even end up committing all your time to the planning process without achieving significant results. Trust me, you're not alone.

To resolve these over-arching issues, it's best to hire creative organizers who have committed their time and lives to planning events for a wide range of clients. Not only will they help you with the important details of what you want your event to look like, but they will also save you time and a headache. Here is why you should make use of professionals.

Should you get involved or not in your event planning?

How much time should you invest in event planning? You have an option of involvement or otherwise.

Depending on what you want, hiring an event pro provides you with two options: get involved or uninvolved in the planning process. Most clients who involve themselves in the planning process will seek every detail – even the minutest ones – of the event planning process.

Your primary objective is to host an event that leaves unforgettable experiences in the minds of attendees. Therefore, it is wise to stay clear so that you are not interfering in the planning process.

With an event planner, all you need is to tell them what you want and the planner will follow your instructions and make their recommendations. The key aspect of planning is that your planner will be available on the day in case something goes wrong.

Event planners save you time, stress, and money.

Event planning is time-consuming – about 200+ hours go into it. You will have to do a balancing act between planning and your competing priorities. For instance, you may need to visit a vendor to negotiate a venue as well as find a trustworthy supplier for items. These dig deep into your time, especially if you're inexperienced. Not only that, you may end up feeling frustrated and spending more money.

But, by giving the pro's a chance to plan your event, you'll save a lot of time. The reason is simple: event planners have a network of 'finders' at their fingertips, they do not need to look for trustworthy vendors. They fill in the gaps and leave you with little or no stress. Through their logistical efforts, they can help you stay within budget.

Did you give it a thought that?

You get to enjoy the event while it last- and be stress-free

There is no way can enjoy an event if you are the planner. This is because you have to keep an eye on all the moving parts of the event to ensure things are running. As an e.g., you need to see if the food service is in order and the technology/entertainment is going as planned, and so on. Like every other guest, you also need to enjoy the party. This is why you need to hire an event planner.

Event planners take on the stress of planning for you. But, event planners are not only experienced at planning events; they are also adept at predicting possible issues – and are, therefore, ready to fix them. They always have a plan B, which they implement in the event things go wrong. This is what makes them a valuable asset as far as event planning is concerned.

Do you want to attract a wider audience?

Hiring an Event Planner allows you the time & flexibility to focus on what matters most to you.

Organizing business events such as product launches, conferences, trade exhibitions, or galas is an excellent way to promote your brand beyond your existing client base. But, you may lack the strategic skills

and experience to organize such an event.

With a professional event planner, you have the time to focus on marketing the event to a wider audience, especially reaching and engaging with your audience, thus meeting your business objectives. Of course, part of what makes an event a success is the marketing efforts of the planner. For instance, a professional event planner will know the right theme and entertainment for your brand. This makes your guests establish an extraordinary connection with your brand.

Key takeaway

The event planning process stretches beyond choosing a venue, food, and vendor (they are important aspects). The event planner facilitates all these, ensuring your event is a success. Their expertise is a value add when it comes to making major decisions that will determine the outcome of your event.

Tight deadlines, physical demands, lack of control, and constant interruptions are common in planning events. While you save money doing it yourself, you save more money when you hand over the planning management in the hands of experts. With this, you are assuring that your event details are being taken care of in a professional manner that synthesizes all aspects to achieve the overall vision.

Do you still need to plan your event yourself? Why not count on the pros to plan your next event – give it a try.

Connect with Lavina: https://www.virtualedgeconnection.com/

THE IMPORTANCE OF RESPECTING YOUR BODY

BY GAIL GENSLER

Body positivity has grown over the last decade or so. We see more and more models and spokespeople with common and relatable body types which is great for inclusivity. As a 60+-year-old pro-aging fitness enthusiast and lifestyle influencer, this movement has helped me tremendously; I keep myself in good shape, but I'm far from perfect like the models we're used to seeing on billboards, magazines, and social media.

These changes have often been boiled down to a specific statement: love your body. This is usually the reasoning behind incorporating more realistic-looking models, doing away with societal and brand stereotyping of what a "model" should look like, and appreciating the unique beauty of every person's body. While the concept of "love your body" is excellent, I have another one that resonates even more deeply with me at this time in my life.

Respect your body.

You Only Have One

When you respect your body, you acknowledge that it is precious. It is, quite literally, your home, and the only one you will ever live in. With this in mind, why wouldn't you treat it with the regard and consideration it deserves?

I respect my body in many different ways. While I still go beast mode in the boxing gym, aging is inevitable. As such, there are certain things I can't do as much of when exercising due to gradual wear and tear. Because of this, I've modified my workouts so I can still get the same results without experiencing pain and exposing myself to a more serious injury. I'm respecting my body by recognizing its limitations and not asking it to do something potentially unsafe. I also eat in a healthful manner, embracing a keto/intermittent fasting lifestyle. If your insides are like the engine in a car, shouldn't you always try to give it the best fuel? I'm not one who measures their food down to the last gram, and I do indulge in keto treats and have my "cheat days" every two weeks (pizza or Mexican are my favorites!) I eat clean. When you respect your body, you give it the nutrients it requires, which will help you look and feel good! I have a wonderful supplement and skincare routine thanks to MDRLabs and Clientele Beauty, and that helps me to take care of my body

from the inside out. I do my best to get proper sleep, hydrate myself properly, and have my "me" time to recharge.

Why We Do It

The "why" is important here. The reason we do what we do. Loving your body is important. Respecting your body? Essential. But who, or what, are you doing it for? Are you doing it because you're simply searching for approval from others? Or are you doing it because you want to live a long, healthy, and disease-free life?

I respect my body because I want to be around- vibrant and healthy- as my daughter progresses through life. I respect my body because I like the feeling of still being able to crush it into my 60s. "Age is just a number" is a common phrase that I use often, but unless I put in the hard work, those are just words.

My actions make them a reality, and they can for you too!

Who's writing: I am sixtypreneur Gail Gensler, changing the narrative around aging through fitness and embracing a healthy lifestyle from a "real woman's " perspective. My core belief is that age should never determine one's lifestyle, appearance, and most certainly what type of workouts you do!.

My goal is to change the narrative around aging so that younger people can realize that it's something to embrace and look forward to and to inspire and motivate my peers to never take their wellness for granted. A vibrant, healthy life is achievable regardless of age!

I believe that age should never affect how we dress, what we enjoy doing, and how we should be portrayed in society. I am here to break down the barriers of institutional ageism and change how brands look at midlife women. We are generally depicted as in need of medication, slowing down, or as a grandmother. I am the antithesis of this-a a perfect example of a vibrant, healthy, active 60-year-old. My preference is to see the items I wish to purchase on someone like me- not a 20-year-old and I am certainly not alone in this viewpoint.

Connect with Gail: www.gailgensler.com

SHOW ME YOUR PRIDE

BY KIM HOPE

Bio:

Kim is a holistic practitioner certified in nutrition, personal training, and essential oils. She believes movement and eating should be for function. To be strong, agile, and free of illness. Kim is a Hashimoto survivor and has Osteopenia (the start of Osteoporosis). After being diagnosed with both at age 50, she started looking for natural ways to heal her body. As she did so also did her passion to help others do the same. Kim sought out education to help others prevent and reverse chronic disease through diet and exercise. She'll never stop learning as science changes every day. Kim now helps many reverse illnesses like diabetes, high blood pressure, and mental illness by helping reduce the inflammation in their bodies. Kim helps people get to the root causes of inflammation and reduce or eliminate medicines. while restoring their health.

July is a month we celebrate with pride the birth of our country. America's birthday. The Red, White, and Blue. The grand old flag, parades, fireworks, and barbeques.

I thought it would be fitting to talk about pride. Pride and wellness that is.

Do you have a car?

I bet as most Americans do, you take pride in that car. You get tires and brake changes, tune-ups, and oil changes. You take it to get washed and waxed and vacuum the inside.

Do you own a home? I bet you take pride in that home. You keep it shoveled in the winter and mowed in the summer. You keep the trim painted. You keep the roof in tip-top shape. You keep the furnace and water heater going.

Each spring I bet you give the house a deep cleaning. You scrub floors, dust, and clean windows. I bet you might even steam clean your carpets and hardwood floors.

You take pride in your material things. You paid good money for them and want them to last. You take pride in the upkeep you do and how well they last and keep working because you invest time and money to keep them optimized.

Pride is defined as a feeling of deep pleasure or satisfaction derived from one's own achievements. For some reason, a lot of people invest more in things than themselves. We go the cheap and fast route on the foods we eat. We look for quantity over quality. How much can we get in until we are full? How much can I eat this weekend than

work off on Monday? How can I starve all day to eat those cookies tonight?

Somewhere along the way, we learned to treat our bodies as expendable, yet we are shocked when diagnosed with an autoimmune disease, high blood pressure, or prediabetic. We refuse to invest in ourselves now taking chances every day with our health yet drive through a car wash to see that shiny new car.

Why do we treat our possessions better than ourselves? Why don't we take pride in our own health?

I'd like to instill the belief that investing in our health pays dividends later. How about living a longer quality of life? How about traveling and going on adventures even at a late age without being held back by illness?

Have you heard the phrase invest in your wellness before you soon invest in your illness?

Prevention of illness should be a number one priority in pride yourself. The only way this is achieved is by living a healthy lifestyle free of chronic inflammation and disease. We achieve this through daily movement, eating a well-balanced diet that is colorful and diverse, and living a stress-free life as much as possible.

Did you know only 12% of Americans are considered metabolically healthy? That's 1 in 8 Americans. Obesity is increasing at an alarming rate. Nearly ½ of all Americans are obese. Obesity leads to obesity-related conditions like heart disease, stroke, type 2 diabetes, and even cancer.

Remember me asking you about the price you pay later for not taking care of our health. In 2008 the medical costs for obesity was $147 billion. During 2020 and 2021 the average weight gain was 15-20 lbs and most people haven't taken that weight off and possibly gained more since.

It's time to take pride in ourselves again. It's time to take a better interest in us rather than things. Because if we aren't around or are too ill that you cannot enjoy your home, car or boat.

When we take care of our health it makes the world a better place.

When we are well, we are happy.

When we are happy, we not only live longer (studies show an average of 10 years longer) but we pour that happiness into others. When you are healthy and feel well you are more likely to socialize and have fun.

When we eat healthier it also aids in sustainability. Especially a plant-forward eating lifestyle. You'll eat less out of a box and more whole foods. This lessens your carbon footprint. Eating more red and processed meats studies show causes most illness and pollution.

When we are well there are fewer medications being flushed through water systems and into drinking water. There is less plastic and waste in landfills.

In a month when we take pride in America and its history, let's get back to taking pride in ourselves and the world around us. The people who we share this country with. Inspire your family and friends to take pride in themselves too.

Happy Birthday America

Go show me your pride.

Hope& Health

Connect with Kim: https://linktr.ee/KimHope

Listen to the latest
Oh my
HEALTH...
There is
HOPE!
Podcast Episode
out now iTunes or Google Play

KNOWLEDGE IS POWER; HORMONAL DISRUPTERS AND TAKING CONTROL

BY DR. FABIANNA MARIE

As a naturopath, my job is to treat, work and educate my patient; mind, body, and soul. The intimate details of my patient's health lies in accounting for previous experience, expectations, education of their own health, beliefs, stress, personality, triggers, social impact, and financial circumstances or burdens. I am essentially a detective who will get to the bottom of your health concerns and put all the pieces of the puzzle together. Together we optimize your whole health by working backward. There is no end result until we can find the root cause of your ailments. Most of the time the answers don't slap me in the face, they lie in the details of our conversations. As a Naturopath, I am privileged to see the rainbow of colors when it comes to my patient's health and wellness. My job is not black and white as seen with most conventional medicine. No two people are the same, which is why no two treatment plans should be either.

In biology, we are taught that our bodies are run by a network of hormones and glands that regulate everything we do. Hormones, such as estrogen, progesterone, testosterone, insulin, and cortisol, are vital chemical messengers that control the body's communication pathways and affect many aspects of overall health. Hormones are secreted by exocrine glands, including but not limited to your adrenals, pituitary gland, ovaries/testes, pancreas, etc. The hormones works together to form one mass communication system, called your endocrine system. Even slight imbalances in these hormones can lead to widespread symptoms, and much like a stone dropped into a lake, even a small disruption can create a ripple effect. The endocrine system plays a starring role in all phases of development, metabolism, and behavior. The big bad truth that most doctors won't ever discuss is exposure to synthetic chemicals in products. Most often we are not aware what any of the chemicals that are plastered on the back of any product. We would all need a Masters in Science to actually understand the plethora of abbreviations, symbols, and words we can't pronounce.

- DDT, Chlorpyrifos, Atrazine, 2, 4-D, Glyphosate
- Pesticides
- Lead, Phthalates, Cadmium
- Chidren's Products
- Polychlorinated biphenyls (PCBs) and Dioxins
- Industrial Solvents or Lubricants and their Byproducts
- Bisphenol A (BPA), Phthalates, Phenol
- Plastics, and Food Storage Materials
- Diethylstilbestrol (DES)
- Pharmaceutical agents

When absorbed in the body, an endocrine disruptor can decrease or increase normal hormone levels, mimic the body's natural hormones, or alter the natural production of hormones. Unfortunately, we are exposed to these chemicals daily, and we're especially vulnerable to them during phases of accelerated development—in utero and throughout our teen years.

As a hormone and autoimmune specialist, as I said earlier, I become a detective of sorts. Some of my patients look at me as if I have three heads when I ask probing questions about their childhood and teen years. What I see in most of my patients who experience difficulty in hormonal health: which includes conceiving a child, miscarriages, cancers linked to hormones such as Breast or Ovarian cancers, is exposure to early hormone disrupters. Looking back to my own childhood there are many things that stick out for me when it came to understanding why I was diagnosed with a debilitating autoimmune disease and Breast Cancer before turning 28. While this is a very heavy topic I want you to know there is someone who understands, has educated herself, and truly wants to help change the trajectory of health care. Conventional management of hormone imbalances are often to replace or suppress, as seen with the birth control pill, thyroid medication, HRT, insulin replacement, and so many others. Unfortunately, for many people this only masks the issue, leading to a dependency on medication while secondary symptoms progress, all while exposing people to risk factors such as stroke, osteoporosis, mood disorders, a lack of sex drive, reproductive issues, and certain cancers.

Signs of symptoms of hormonal imbalances may include, but are not limited to:

Adrenal Fatigue: fatigue, brain fog, low sex drive, hypothyroid symptoms, trouble sleeping, anxiety, difficulty losing weight, low motivation

Estrogen Excess: PMS, mood swings, weight gain around the hips, water retention, heavy menses, hypothyroid symptoms, nervousness, sweet cravings, low libido, hair loss

Estrogen Deficiency: Hot flashes, night sweats, irritability, depression, nervousness, decreased libido, urinary incontinence, heart palpitations, foggy thinking, sleep disturbances, memory lapses, hair loss, dry skin, vaginal atrophy, vaginal dryness

Progesterone Deficiency: PMS, mood swings, infertility, water retention, fibrocystic breasts, irritability/nervousness, sweet cravings, hypothyroid symptoms, low libido

Insulin Resistance/Excess: weight gain, nerve damage, increased urination, dry mouth, PCOS

Androgen excess: acne, hirsutism, weight issues, irregular/absent menses, hair loss

Androgen deficiency: erectile dysfunction, muscle loss, weight gain, fatigue, mood-related problems

Thyroid Dysfunction: hypothyroidism, hyperthyroidism, goiters, thyroid nodules, and autoimmune thyroid disorders: Grave's Disease, Hashimoto's thyroid

The tedious nature of managing hormone imbalances is to first and foremost uncover the discrepancy, and work towards recovery by using the many tools and vastness provided by nature to balance out endogenous production of the necessary hormone, all while the speeding movement of excesses through the liver. The saying, "Knowledge is power" has become my mantra for thriving with two diagnosis' that could have ended my life seventeen years ago. Becoming a Naturopath and the education I continue to arm myself with has been such a gift to my own health, but also to the many patients I get the honor to work with. The deep dive into your own health can be a tedious and scary process if you don't have someone who can help you navigate. Doctor Google is never a route to lay the groundwork for curing any ailment. Symptoms are not enemies to be destroyed, but sacred messengers who encourage us to take better care of ourselves. Today's article I hope to be a reminder and encouragement to seek what is holding you back from your optimal health. It is never too late to start living your best life.

Namaste- Dr. Fab

Connect with Dr. Fabianna:

https://linktr.ee/Drfab

HOW TO TIMELINE HOP

BY CASSIDY REY

Do you feel like your life is slow progressing or stagnant? Well, I have a trick for you to help you get out of this funk. It is called Timeline Hopping. I am a Young Professional Psychic/Medium & Reiki Master and Timeline Hopping is something I help teach my clients to use to their advantage. Here are 4 ways you can do this on your own;

1. Be present: The only way you're ever going to be able to openly receive the blessings that are trying to enter your life is by being present. That simply means NOTHING in this world except for RIGHT NOW matters. You reading this sentence is all you have in this world at this moment. You cannot get stuck in the "what if" narrative of thinking back to your past or forward to your unpredictable future. The truth is, you're creating your future as you read this. You slow your own timeline down by having this mindset of worry or regret. Let it go, let it flow, release control.

2. Show gratitude: Another way you can Timeline Hop is by showing gratitude for the HERE & NOW. If you are not grateful for what you presently have then you are never going to be satisfied with what you are wishing for. When you think of the things you want in this life are you searching just for a material item? No, you are searching for the feeling that that item will bring you. Of course, we all want a big house, copious amounts of money, the lifestyle to travel. But why do we want it? We want it because we think when we have it we will FINALLY be happy. Plot twist...that's a lie this society taught you. Start focusing on the feeling you're searching for because I guarantee you that is a feeling you can find right now in the present. Are you looking for happiness? Okay, then think about what makes you smile, who makes you smile, why they make you smile, and BE GRATEFUL for that. You know happiness, you know sadness, you know grief, these are all emotions you are aware of and have felt before. So the only thing holding you back from your manifestations is your mindset of wanting more of what you don't have when it is accessible to you RIGHT NOW.

3. Stay In Alignment: So now that you are practicing being present and showing gratitude, why are your manifestations still not happening? The reason is that you are not acting in accordance with what your soul truly wants. Staying in alignment means living authentically. If you are causing harm to yourself or others in any way, this is not congruent with what you are manifesting. For example, if you want to save up for a house but are recklessly spending money on materialistic items, that is not in alignment with your goals. If you do not live in accordance with what you envision for yourself then you will never get where you want to be. Think, speak, and act in alignment with your soul's wants and needs.

4. Visualize: The last step is visualization. There are many techniques out there but what I would recommend is to journal. What you want to do is visualize yourself in that new house, creating your happy family, making that new friend, etc. And think about that thing or that person like it is already PRESENTLY available to you and happening in your life. This is truly the most important step to Timeline Hopping because it allows you to create a new reality in your mind. It is not done in a way where you are overthinking about the future and worrying about "how" to get there, you are simply sitting in a space of acceptance. You see that vision, you feel it, you understand what it means to you, and you write it down on a piece of paper. Talk about the details of your new home. What does your office look like? Your backyard? Do you have neighbors or is it secluded? Go there and run with it.

If you practice these steps on a daily/weekly basis I guarantee you your life will start to change and you will see your manifestations come to life faster than you could've ever imagined. Be present, show gratitude, stay in alignment, and visualize into the life you deserve! It is waiting for you.

Connect with Cassidy: https://linktr.ee/cass__reyy

Meet Cassidy

How much do you love lemongrass?

GET READY TO FIND OUT WHY YOU SHOULD BE STOCKING UP ON THIS WONDER OIL!

Lemongrass oil comes with a variety of properties such as analgesic, antibacterial, anticancer, anti-inflammatory, antiseptic, insect repellant, revitalize, sedative, tonic, and vasodilator.

Eye Health Support

Lemongrass helps promote awareness and release mental fatigue. It has been shown to aid in improved vision, reduces muscular dystrophy, retina strengthening, reducing sprains or strains, while repairing tissue, wounds, and improving ligament strength. Lemongrass helps get the oxygen flowing which is essential for eye health support.

Vasodilator

When it comes to supporting your health circulation is key to improving eye health. Lemongrass is a natural diuretic that helps eliminate edema and fluid retention. It is a natural anti-inflammatory, revitalization, sedative, and vasodilator. Lemongrass' ability to strengthen vascular walls allows for the strengthening of blood flow and circulation to vital areas such as eye health.

Air Purifier

Unlike other organs, our eyes are constantly exposed to the elements. Regrettably, our air and environment are not always the best. Luckily, lemongrass is a natural antibacterial, antiseptic, and insect repellent. Its natural ability to remove air pollution and eliminate airborne bacteria makes it a must to support eye health and respiratory health.

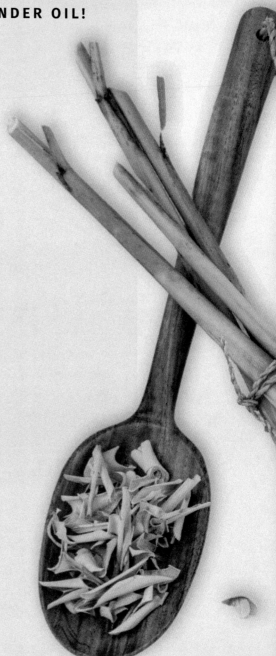

Refreshed and Invigorating Scrub:

1 cup Epsom Salt

5 drops Peppermint Essential oil

4 drops Lavender Essential oil

1 cup Raw Coconut Oil

6 drops grapefruit Essential oil

8 drops Vitamin E oil

6 drops Lemongrass Essential Oil

Directions:

Into a bowl combine all ingredients and mix well together.

Transfer the mixture into a container and use it regularly.

If you are looking for a bath salt to soak into remove the coconut oil from the mix and use 1-2 tablespoons per bath.

SHIFT YOUR PERSPECTIVE ON YOURSELF AND BODY TO BE HAPPY

BY NATHALIE BOTROS

Sometimes we don't see the importance of the words that we use or the power of our thoughts. We are our biggest critics, and we don't understand that those negative words take away our joy and happiness.

Don't worry I got you covered, I will explain to you how to shift your perspective on yourself and your body to be happy? How to change your words and thoughts. It takes a little work but has so much impact on your wellbeing.

What do I mean by shifting your perspective? Very simple:

Imagine you have a camera, or your phone and you are trying to take that amazing picture. The problem is the image you see is not good: maybe it is a little blurry or the light doesn't look good. What do you do? You change the settings until the image you see looks good. Correct?

Let's do this with yourself and your body. Imagine the camera is your thoughts and the image is you and/or your body. When you look at yourself what do you see? Do you see an amazing, accomplished woman or a failure?

What about when you look at your body? Do you see the beautiful woman you are or do you think you should change something: lose/gain weight, change your hair or even have surgery to fix your image?

Shifting your perspective is focusing the camera on the positive. Tuning your thoughts so you see the positive, the happy, the beautiful, and the amazing. You have different ways to do it.

The first one is "Find the positive in all flaws and turn them into qualities"

I know it seems hard to find the positive in our negative thoughts, but let's play a game:

I want to write on a piece of paper 5 flaws about yourself, it can be physical or mental.

The exercise is to find the positive aspect of each flaw.

A very common example with my patients is the sentence "I need to lose weight". We all want to lose or gain weight, what about changing it to "I have some extra weight, which makes my body curvy and sexy." Also another way of seeing it is: More weight means, more of me to love.

Another example would be "I am shy". Let's change the wording and say I am mysterious. Saying the word and thinking about it will definitely change the energy you emit and attract the right people.

We all have so many insecurities that we define as flaws, but they are just in our heads. We should let those insecurities block our happiness, define them, change how we describe them as much as we want until they become a quality. As you can see, you can always find the positive side to any negative thought about yourself and your body, you just need to play with the word a little until you love the outcome.

The second one is "Stop thinking with the world "Should"

Every time you say I "should be" this skinny, that smart, with that hair color and that confidence... you condition your happiness.

For example: If you think: "I should be a size 2 to be happy", you are conditioning your happiness to that number. But if you say I am a size 2, 10, or 16 and I love every inch of my body. You shift your words, your thoughts, and the outcome.

Avoid using I should, and set yourself free of this conditioned happiness

The third one is "Use positive words"

Talking about the words we use, did you ever think about the words that you use when you talk or write? Do you describe positive or negative words? Sometimes changing one word can change the whole energy of the sentence and therefore your energy which will create a happier life for you. Think about it...

If you spend your day saying I am stressed, your body listens to you and will become stressed. If you change the word stress into excitement, your statement would be I am excited. You change the energy of the statement.

Another word that you should definitely change is "failure", replace it with "learned a lesson". So, instead of thinking you failed, you say I've learned a lesson. This would help you to try again, and use what you learned on your second, third, or fourth trial.

Another important word that you should be careful using is "I have to". Replace it with "I get to". For example, if you describe your day by saying "I have to work", it comes out negative as punishment. If you describe it with "I get to work", the meaning is positive, as you are lucky enough to work.

We believe talking to plants makes them grow faster and give better fruits. If this theory is correct; imagine how much you will grow, be happy and emit amazing energy if you use positive words to talk about yourself. Those good words will be in your thoughts, and you will be happy unconditionally!

Connect with Nathalie: https://linktr.ee/nathaliebotros

How much do you like the body you are in?

Meet Nathalie

TRANSFORMATION

BY MICHELLE FULLER

Five years ago, I found myself in a sea of tissues under the covers on my bed. At the time, I was in my early forties. I had just ended a long-term relationship. My boyfriend sat on my couch one night and told me he wasn't ready to marry me. He said he didn't know if he would ever be ready. I had wanted the relationship to end for over a year, but never had the strength to do it. I was finally free, or so I thought. Less than a week later, I found myself in my bed hiding from the world. I felt completely alone. Why had I stayed with someone who treated me so badly? Why had I stayed in a relationship that I didn't want to be in? What was I going to do now? Questions flooded my mind.

I thought about my failures. I thought about my two divorces. I thought about everything I had settled for in life and love. The pain was crippling. I felt defeated. I was in the middle of a mid-life crisis. I was halfway through my life and I felt I had nothing to show for it.

I reached out to a relationship coach for help. I was desperate for some kind of relief. I needed to figure out what was holding me back. He emailed me some forms to complete about myself and my past. I sat on the floor pouring over them writing down everything I could remember about my childhood. It was long and mentally draining.

On our first Zoom call, my coach told me...

"You are trying to work out the relationship you had with your Mom in your romantic relationships. You attract people to you that act like her or treat you the same way she did."

My Mom passed away when I was 14. I had tucked her away in the back corner of my mind. I rarely discussed her or my memories of her. The memories I did have were full of heartbreak and I avoided them at all costs.

My Mom grew up poor in a rural Kentucky town. My grandparents were alcoholics and spent most of their time partying. My grandmother was emotionally abusive and did not love or nurture my Mom. She had little time or patience for her and made that clear in her words and actions.

My Mom married my Dad right after she graduated from high school. My Dad had a new job with the telephone company in Lexington and bought them a new home. 5 years later, I was born. My sister was born less than 2 years later. They appeared to have a picture-perfect family. Looks are always deceiving.

While my Mom made her escape from her childhood home, she didn't leave her past. She carried the demons of her childhood with her until she died.

My Mom and I had a toxic relationship. I was never close to her. She was hard to get along with and I did my best to stay out of her way. She had no patience for me and I never felt safe sharing my feelings with her. She never told me she loved me. I never heard that I was smart or beautiful. She yelled her way through each day, full of rage. She spent most of her weekends going out with friends while my Dad watched my sister and me.

My parents separated when I was 10. My Mom had an affair with a neighbor and moved into an apartment on the other side of town. I hated spending time with my Mom. I moved my things out of her apartment one weekend on the heels of an argument with her. I swore I would never return.

My Mom moved back in less than 6 months later. She had breast cancer and they had not caught the disease in time. She died 4 years later at the age of 36.

My Mom had shown up in every part of my life. I had yearned for her love when she was alive. I never felt like she saw me or heard me. I was full of rage and resentment when I thought of her. I had no idea that resentment was the very thing standing in my way.

That was the day I met The Burn.

The Burn is all the things I avoided in life. It's the things we all avoid. My burn was my past, forgiveness, and taking responsibility for my life and actions.

I had to face the things I didn't want to deal with. I had to deal with things that I had pushed down and away to the far corners of my mind.

I started to heal with each new day. I faced my past. I forgave my Mom and each person who had ever hurt me. I took responsibility for my life and actions.

Less than 6 months later, I sold my house and moved to Austin. I met my fiance less than 2 years later and created an incredible relationship with him. I started coaching other people on transformation and The Burn. My entire life changed in one moment. Sometimes, we need someone to open the window to our minds so we can see what we have avoided. Change is born in pain, but change is available whenever we are ready.

Connect with Michelle: https://linktr.ee/oneboldmf

SUMMER FOODS, TO HELP YOU THRIVE!

Gluten-Free   Vegan   Dairy-Free

JALAPENO STUFFED CHICKEN

Serves 4

1 egg beaten

1/4 cup gluten-free flour

3 ounces vegan cream cheese

1 cup vegan shredded cheddar cheese

1/2 cup vegan shredded pepper jack cheese

3 jalapenos seeded and minced

1 clove garlic minced

2 Tbsp vegan butter

4 boneless skinless chicken breasts

2 Tbsp Olive Oil

Corn:

2 Tbsp Olive Oil

4 ears corn kernels removed from the cob

1/4 cup green onions chopped

1/2 tsp chili powder

2 Tbsp vegan mayo

3/4 cup vegan feta cheese

1/2 cup cilantro chopped

juice and zest of 1 lime

1 Tbsp tajin

Directions:

Place the egg into one bowl and flour into another bowl for dredging (shallow bowls are best). Prepare the filling by combining cream cheese, cheeses, jalapeno, garlic, and salt. Make sure to season the flour mixture as well. Cut the chicken through the middle horizontally without cutting all the way through. Open the chicken and fill with 1-2 tablespoons of the filling. Close the chicken, dredge both sides of the chicken into the egg, and then the flour mixture.

Into a large skillet heat the oil, corn, chives, and seasonings. Cook until the corn has softened. Remove the corn from the heat and combine with the remaining ingredients in a bowl then set aside. Cook the chicken in the same skillet with oil and butter. Brown the chicken for 3-4 minutes on each side or until golden brown on all sides. Remove from heat, and sprinkle the remaining cheese and jalapenos over the chicken. Place under the broil for 1-2 minutes or until the cheeses have melted. Serve the chicken with corn, cilantro, and lime juice on top.

NO-BAKE ALMOND BUTTER PIE

Serves 12

Crust:

1/4 cup Agave Syrup

2 cups Almond Flour

1/4 cup Unsweetened Cocoa Powder

1 tsp Pure Vanilla

1/4 cup Raw Coconut Oil melted

Filling:

1 cup Almond Butter

2 Tbsps Chia Seeds (ground)

1/3 cup Agave Syrup

1 1/4 cup Coconut Milk Full-Fat

1/3 cup Coconut Cream

1/4 cup Raw Coconut Oil Melted

Directions:

Preheat the oven to 350 degrees F. In a large bowl, combine flour, cocoa, oil, syrup, and vanilla. Use your hands to combine all the ingredients together. Pretreat a 9-inch pie dish with a non-stick preventative of choice and press dough into the pan. Bake the crust for 15-20 minutes or you can freeze the crust for 1-2 hours for a frozen delight. Meanwhile, prepare the filling. In a blender, combine all the filling ingredients and mix on high until it forms into a thick sticky paste.

If you choose to bake the crust let cool completely before spreading the filling into the pie evenly. Refrigerate for at least 30 minutes then top with dark chocolate drizzle and fresh almond butter drizzle. Serve chilled or frozen based on preference.

CANTALOUPE MARGARITA

Serves 2

1 cantaloupe cubbed and frozen

Juice of 2 limes

2 tsp Agave Syrup

1/2 cup Ice

1 Coconut Lime Bia Water

*For the Adult version add 2 oz Tequila for each person

Directions:

Combine all ingredients into a blender and blend until desired texture has been reached. Pour into a glass of choice and top with sugar (monk fruit works well) rim and either a lime wedge or slice of cantaloupe.

GINGER PEACH BOURBON THYME

Serves 1

1/2 lemon juiced

1 Tbsp Maple Syrup

1/2 cup fresh peach slices

4 sprigs of thyme fresh

2 oz bourbon

1 ginger beer

Directions:

Combine all ingredients into a glass and stir well. For added chill during the hotter days freeze the peaches. For a non-alcoholic option swap the ginger ale.

FIG BREAD

Serves 12

3 Large Eggs

2-2 1/2 cups Coconut Sugar

3/4 cup Raw Coconut Oil melted

2 cups Ripe Figs Mashed

1 cup Almond Flour

2 cups Oat Flour

1 tsp Salt

2 tsp Baking Soda

1/2 cup Vegan Buttermilk, well shaken

1 cup pecans chopped

1/2 tsp cinnamon ground

Directions:

Preheat the oven to 350 degrees F. Pretreat a 9x13 inch baking dish with a non-stick option of choice. Into a mixing bowl combine the sugar and eggs. At a low speed mix the figs and oil into the egg mixture. Into a separate bowl combine flour, baking soda, salt, and cinnamon. Add the flour mixture into the egg mixture and alternate with vegan buttermilk. Beat until well combined. Fold in chopped pecans and bake for 50-60 minutes or until a toothpick comes out clean.

BLACK CURRANT CUPCAKES

Serves 12

3 cups black currants

1/3 cup vegan butter room temp

3/4 cup coconut sugar

1 cup Coconut flour

1/2 cup almond flour

3 large eggs

1 tsp Baking powder

Directions:

Preheat the oven to 350 degrees F. Pretreat a cupcake pan with your choice of non-stick option (I use parchment paper cups). Clean and dry the black currants. Into a large bowl cream together the butter and sugar until well combined. Add eggs in one at a time until well incorporated. Into another bowl combine the flours and baking powder. Mix well. Using a sifter slowly incorporate the dry ingredients into the wet. Once the batter is well combined pour it into the cupcake holders. Make sure to leave room for the currants. Top the batter with currants and bake for 30-40 minutes or until a toothpick comes out clean. Let cool in pan for 5-10 minutes prior to transferring onto a wire rack to cool completely.

RASPBERRY CRUMBLE BARS

Makes 20 Bars

Crumble:

1 cup Vegan butter cold cubed

2 cups Oats

1 cup Oat Flour

1/2 cup Almond Flour

1 cup Coconut Sugar

1/2 tsp Cinnamon ground

1 tsp Baking Powder

Filling:

2 1/2 cups Fresh Raspberries

1/2 cup Raspberry Chia Jam

2 Tbsp Pure Vanilla

1 Ripe Peach sliced thin

2 Tbsp Oat Flour

3 Tbsp Lemon Zest

2-4 Tbsp Coconut Sugar

Directions:

Preheat the oven to 350 degrees and retreat a 9x13 inch baking dish with a non-stick option of choice. Into a food processor, pulse together oats, flour, sugar, baking powder, and cinnamon until the oats are mostly ground. Add the cold butter and pulse until a crumbly dough forms. If the dough seems too dry add 1 Tbsp water. Press 1/3 of the dough into the baking dish and bake for 10 minutes or until lightly golden.

Meanwhile, in a medium bowl toss the raspberries with sugar, flour, zest, and vanilla. Spread the berries out evenly over the prebaked crust. Dollop the jam over the berries and add peach slices over the berries. Sprinkle the remaining dough over the top and bake for an additional 30-40 minutes or until the crumble is a light golden color. Allow cooling completely before cutting into bars.

ZUCCHINI PUFFS

Serves 24

3/4 cup Buckwheat Flour

2 tsp Italian Seasoning

3/4 Coconut Milk

1 egg

3/4 tsp Baking Powder

1 cup Grated Zucchini

1/2 cup shredded vegan cheddar cheese

salt and pepper to taste

Directions:

Add salt to the grated zucchini and drain excess water from the zucchini. In a large bowl, combine the flour, powder, and seasoning. Into a small bowl, combine the milk and egg. Then add the egg mixture to the dry ingredients and mix well. Add the shredded zucchini and cheese to the batter and spoon them into a muffin pan. Bake in a preheated 375-degree oven for 20 minutes or until the center is done.

GREEN BEANS ALMONDINE

Serves 4

1 pound French Green Beans trimmed

2 Tbsp Vegan Butter

1/4 cup Raw Sliced Almonds

2 medium Shallots diced

zest and juice of 1 lemon

2 cloves garlic minced

salt and pepper to taste

1 cup vegan parmesan

Directions:

Blanch the green beans for 4-5 minutes (boil then place directly into ice water to shock beans). Meanwhile, in a large skillet, melt butter and saute almonds for 2-3 minutes or until golden. Reduce the heat to low and add the shallots and garlic. Saute for an additional 1-2 minutes stirring frequently. Transfer the green beans into the skillet and saute until tender. Add in the juice and zest seasoning to taste. Top with vegan parmesan and serve hot.

BITTER MELON STIR FRY

Serves 4

1 pound bitter melon sliced

1/2 tsp chili pepper flakes

1 Tbsp minced garlic

2 Tbsp Sesame Oil

1 Tbsp Rice Wine Vinegar

2 Tbsp Coconut Amino

1/2 tsp Coconut Sugar

2 medium Carrots cubed

1 Shallot minced

1/2 red cabbage shredded

1 broccoli stalk cubed

2 cloves garlic minced

Directions:

Into a large skillet heat oil, garlic, and shallots. Once fragrant, saute carrots, melon, and broccoli stalk. Add in seasonings and saute for 3-5 minutes or until tender. Lastly, add cabbage and cook for another 1-2 minutes. Serve over rice.

NECTARINE CAKE

Serves 14

Cake:

1 cup Coconut flour

1/4 cup almond flour

1/3 cup vegan butter

1/2 cup coconut sugar

1 egg

pinch of salt

1 Tbsp cornmeal

2 3/4 cups nectarines

Topping:

3 eggs

4 Tbsp Stevia Monk Fruit

3 Tbsp almond flour

Directions:

Preheat the oven to 400 degrees F. Pretreat an 8x13 inch baking dish with a non-stick option of choice. Into a food processor combine flour, butter, sugar, salt, and egg. Mix until the dough starts to come together. The dough should be wet but not sticky, if too sticky add a tablespoon of additional flour. Press the dough into the pan and bake until lightly golden. Meanwhile, clean, remove the pits, and cut them into wedges. Remove the cake from the oven and sprinkle evenly with cornmeal. Arrange nectarine slices over the top and bake for an additional 10 minutes.

To prepare the topping separate egg whites. Beat the egg whites until stiff. Mix together yolks and sugar. Once well combined mix the flour into the yolk mixture. Fold in the beaten egg whites. Pour this mixture over the cake and continue to bake for another 15 minutes or until golden brown.

GREEK CHICKEN ORZO WITH TOMATOES

Serves 6

4 Tbsp Olive Oil

1 pound Boneless, skinless chicken, cubbed

1/2 cup fresh oregano chopped

2 tsp Paprika

4 cloves garlic minced

2 Tbsp Balsamic vinegar

1 bell pepper sliced

2 cups orzo pasta

1 cup olives pitted

salt and pepper to taste

1 cup vegan feta cheese

Tomatoes:

2 cups heirloom tomatoes chopped

1/3 cup olive oil

3 cloves garlic minced

1/3 cup fresh basil chopped

Directions:

Using a large skillet toss together with olive oil, chicken, oregano, paprika, salt, and pepper. Over medium-high heat cook until the chicken is browned and cooked through. Stir in the balsamic and garlic. Cook for an additional minute and remove from the skillet. Into the now-empty skillet, add the bell peppers and cook for 2-3 minutes. Once soft, add in orzo and 2 1/2 cups of water. Season with salt and pepper. Cook until almost all the water is absorbed, about 10 minutes. Transfer the chicken and olives into the orzo.

Once the chicken is warmed through, about 3 minutes. Meanwhile, toss all the ingredients for the tomatoes together into a bowl. Season with salt and pepper. To serve, spoon the tomatoes over the chicken and gently toss. Top with feta and more fresh herbs.

BEET & KOHLRABI SLAW

Serves 4

1 large kohlrabi peeled and shredded

2 medium raw beets peeled and shredded

1 apple cored and cut into matchsticks

2 Tbsp parsley minced

Juice and zest of 1 orange

2 green onions chopped

1 lime juiced

2 carrots shredded

1/2 red cabbage shredded

2 Tbsp avocado oil

1/4 cup toasted sunflower seeds

1 Tbsp Apple cider vinegar

salt and pepper to taste

Vegan feta cheese (optional)

Directions:

Into a large bowl combine all fruits and vegetables and give a light toss. To prepare the dressing, into a small bowl whisk together juice, vinegar, oil, salt, and pepper. Once whisked together pour over slaw and toss. Top with seeds and feta if desired.

SPICY TURKEY TACO SALAD

Serves 4

2 Tbsp Avocado Oil

1 pound ground lean turkey

3 tsp Chili Powder

1 Tbsp smoked paprika

1/3 cup cilantro chopped

1 1/2 tsp ground cumin

6 cups dark leafy greens

1 tsp garlic powder

3/4 cup vegan cheddar cheese

1 cup black beans

2 jalapenos thinly chopped

1 mango diced

2 avocadoes cubbed

3 cups fresh cut corn

salt and pepper to taste

corn tortilla chips

2 tsp honey

1/4 cup cilantro chopped

1 jalapeno seeded, minced

2 Tbsp chives chopped

salt and pepper to taste

Dressing:

1 cup vegan greek yogurt

2 limes juiced

1 Tbsp apple cider vinegar

Directions:

Heat the oil in a large skillet over medium heat. Season to taste and brown the meat. Remove from heat and drain excess grease from the meat. While the meat cools in a large bowl combine all remaining ingredients for the salad. In a small bowl mix together the ingredients for the dressing. Add the meat and toss the salad in the dressing. For added crunch add toasted pumpkin seeds.

STRAWBERRY WATERMELON SORBET

Serves 12

1/2 large seedless watermelon cubed, frozen

10 strawberries wedged, frozen

2 Tbsp lime juice

Directions:

Into a blender combine all ingredients and blend until smooth. Pour mixture into a freezer-friendly container and let freeze for 1-2 hours.

KOREAN CAULIFLOWER LETTUCE WRAPS

Serves 6

1 large cauliflower cut into florets

2 Tbsp olive oil

butter lettuce cups

1/2 cup chopped cashews

Green Onions chopped

Sauce:

1/2 cup coconut amino

1 Tbsp rice vinegar

1/4 cup coconut sugar

1 Tbsp gochujang

2 cloves garlic minced

1 inch fresh ginger minced

1/2 Tbsp cornstarch

1 Tbsp sesame oil

Directions:

Preheat the oven to 450 degrees F. Toss the cauliflower in oil, salt, and pepper to taste. Roast for 30 minutes. Meanwhile, put together all the ingredients for the sauce into a blender. Mix until smooth and transfer into a sauce pot to reduce. Pour the sauce directly over the cauliflower and toss gently to combine. Arrange the wraps based on personal preference and top with nuts, green onions, and additional shredded vegetables.

RADIANT, YOUNGER-LOOKING SKIN

SKIN AND THE CONDITION YOU'RE IN!

BY PAT RILEY & SHERYL WILSON

Ahh to feel free again! Many of us are taking off the face masks, (as the CDC says it is now safe in certain areas). That's great news! We need the connection of social interaction and looking at each other's expressions and faces is part of the joy of living!

Over the pandemic, our lives and routines have changed. Many of us have opted for dressing in more casual clothes, comfy shoes, and wearing less makeup too. With masks off, our skin condition is there for the world to see! Is your skin glowing? Healthy? Firm and even-toned? Or, is it dull, drab, and lacking elasticity? Do you see lines and blemishes in the mirror that make you self-conscious? Is your skin texture smooth or do you struggle with large pores? Would you say your skin is in good shape? To achieve good skin, these first three things must be combined: finding a highly advanced science-based skin care line and working to get your body and mind into a healthy state!

HOW DOES THAT HAPPEN?

People have begun to recognize that our skin mirrors our internal health and general well-being. What you see on the outside is a definite reflection of what is going on inside. Are you eating enough fruits and vegetables? Are you getting enough water for natural detoxification? How about fiber for regular elimination? Do you get the protein you need to build and repair cells?

How positive is your attitude? Increased awareness of our stress and emotions has taught us that self-care, is a necessary part of our daily lives. Here are a few ways to see positive changes in the mirror and in your health:

MAKE YOUR SKIN HAPPIER!

Nutrition and skin care go hand in hand. Your activity level is also key, as movement stimulates circulation, carrying nutrients to every cell in your body. Your exercise routine can be as simple as enjoying daily happy activities. Share experiences with a bestie, your partner, neighbor, or your loving companion.... your dog! Start a new Exercise Class. Have a Spa Day. Take a walk or go on a hike and top it off with a fun picnic at the lake or beach. Get on the treadmill and read that book that you have been wanting to read for forever. Worship. Sing. Belly Dance. Salsa Dance. Zipline, Plant a garden, Volunteer your time to someone or a cause that needs your help. All of these will increase your activity level and make your skin happier because YOU are happier! There truly is a correlation between being happy and peaceful and having healthy, gorgeous skin, hair, and nails and better health!

MORE SELF CARE: BEAUTY IN AND OUT

If you are not happy with your skin condition, now is the time to start a new skin care program! If you get to run down and don't have the stamina you should, perhaps it's time to improve your diet and begin a new supplement program. If you choose to do a cosmetic procedure, speak with your doctor about the various options.

BEFORE AND AFTER THE TREATMENT ROOM!

If you are going to do a Cosmetic Procedure, whether, Invasive or Non-Invasive, plan your pre-treatment and post-treatment, for optimum results. Your doctor will guide you on what supplements to avoid. For example, nutrients that act as blood thinners such as Vitamin E, Turmeric, Garlic, Gingko Biloba, Cranberry, etc. What will your post-procedure self-care involve? Preparing to recover well in advance will improve the value of your treatment and your results.

HOW TO CHOOSE THE RIGHT SKIN CARE AND SUPPLEMENTS TO EMBRACE YOUR INDIVIDUAL NEEDS.

More and more consumers are being driven toward science-based skin care and supplements. Your underlying health is becoming more important than just the outside appearance. For best results, you need a Specialist to investigate your lifestyle and your internal stressors and external stressors and then the fun truly begins! Once you have a Specialist you can trust, you've got a gift that keeps on giving! The Specialist will ask you questions and tailor the skin care and supplements you need over time. You are uniquely you and your conditions change frequently! Perhaps, you've moved to another region that has a different climate, changed your job, are under personal stress, are traveling more frequently, developed a medical condition requiring medications, or have an interrupted sleep pattern. You get the drift! You must pay attention to all that is going on inside to get the optimum results on the outside. The health of your skin, hair, and nails, reflects your internal health.

A Specialist can help guide you, so you know what to do. Then, take a deep breath and jump in! Aspire to grow, evolve, and change every day of your life, to keep it interesting, and challenging so you stay young in mind, spirit, and body!!!

Connect with Clientele: https://www.clientelebeauty.com/

How Well Do You Know Your Skin? Quiz

STOP THE TOXIC!

BY THERESA BYRNE

"I'm miserable! I'm dealing with the world's most toxic person and it's stressing me out! I can't function, I'm not sleeping well, and now my hair is starting to fall out! I can't take it! "

"None of this is my issue but I'm the one who has to deal with it!"

I wish that I could tell you I made that up, but unfortunately, I see this more and more in my coaching practice. Oh, and I've been there too.

In the past few years labeling someone as toxic has become a catch-all for people we don't like, don't get along with, or who (gasp) don't like us. Basically any relationship not working, the other person gets slapped with the toxic label.

It's important we take a deeper look at what the idea of "toxic" means and how it applies. Or doesn't.

Relationships can be toxic, not just people.

Studying social work and psychology in college helped me develop a base of knowledge, and working with over forty-thousand clients directly, I've identified varying patterns in human behavior. Uncovering these patterns in toxicity helps clients move forward.

Without understanding what toxic means, what it looks like, how it feels, and what we can do about it - we are doomed to remain relatively powerless. Why? Because here's the big secret: defining someone else as toxic means it's not your issue. It means you are essentially blameless. "It's not my fault, they are horrible and I am justified in my actions/thoughts/behaviors."

"She is a toxic person - everyone thinks so."

With this thinking, you are at the mercy of someone else.

When a difficulty or challenge isn't yours, you have no power to make changes. The power and control lie in the hands of the other person, not you. When you have no power to change a situation, you remain helpless and stuck in that cycle. Do you see where I'm going with this? Blaming someone else or calling them toxic doesn't allow us the freedom to make different choices. Or do my all-out favorite thing in the world: SET BOUNDARIES!

Side note: No level of abuse is acceptable. Abusers are considered toxic - they cause harm to us. This isn't what I'm talking about here, I'm talking about relationships that aren't working for you.

If you are in an abusive relationship – please reach out for help: https://ncadv.org/resources.

What Is Toxic?

When teaching workshops I define it like this: "Imagine there's a food you're allergic to, or really don't like. For me, it's cilantro (tastes like soap). What happens when you eat this food? You develop a bad reaction from itchy or icky (cilantro!) to life-threatening. This food essentially becomes a kind of poison to your system, on a scale from low to high danger."

Now, is that food toxic? Not to everyone. Some people LOVE cilantro! For years I couldn't figure out how they liked soapy-tasting foods, then it turned out it didn't taste awful to everyone. Just a few of us share a gene - called OR6A2.

Back to you.

Imagine a person you'd define as "toxic" to you.

What do you feel around them?

Where do you feel it in your body?

What "symptoms" do you see?

What "symptoms" do you get around this person?

Many of my clients in a relationship with someone toxic TO THEM will start to develop certain symptoms, as being around this person puts them in a low or high level of distress.

My clients report gaining weight as their bodies produce cortisol (and other adrenal chemicals) against a threat (or donuts sound really good when you're dealing with stress and your brain craves glucose as quick energy)!

They report developing digestive issues. They say they're exhausted, drained, upset, or overwhelmed. Brain fog is common, as are sleep issues. Imagine your body in a level of fight, flight, or freeze whenever you're around this person. What if they aren't toxic to everyone, but they are to your system. They cause harm to your system (emotional, physical, mental, etc) and your sanity. You are essentially allergic to certain people!

It makes sense when you see how some people you'd define as toxic seem to have friends or relationships or success and you can't figure out how they function with others when you cannot stand them.

It might be a particular relationship, or it might be people who tend to have certain views or ways of dealing with life, or it might be how someone treats you that makes it toxic to you.

By removing the idea a person is toxic, and a relationship might be instead, you can then make different choices moving forward.

What can you do about it?

The best advice is to figure out what gets triggered in you when you're around this person, and what about them is toxic to you. Something in your system gets upset, and learning your own self-defeating patterns can help: https://www.theresabyrne.com/mental-fitness-assessment

The next step involves learning how to set boundaries on your time, trust, energy, and exposure to that person. If you can't remove them from your life, at least learn basic boundary-setting skills: www.BoundaryUniversity.com

Reach out to get help to clear your system and your life from the toxicity, you are worth it!

Connect with Theresa: https://theresabyrne.taplink.ws

3-WAYS TO BE IRRESISTIBLE IN YOUR LEADERSHIP

(AND EVERYWHERE ELSE)

BY AMY GERHARTZ

Have you ever seen someone walk into a room and just completely captivate it? It's almost as if they have a certain aura about them that becomes irresistible to everyone in their presence. Have you ever wondered how in the world they do it? Or an even better question, how you could harness and own that power too? There are a few fundamental things that every single alluring person has in order to stand out from the rest of the pack, and it has nothing to do with the clothes they wear, the car they drive, or how much money they have in the bank. What truly makes someone irresistible is their confidence, their self-awareness, and their authenticity. Their ability to be themselves in any situation is what truly sets them apart, and is what will set you apart as well.

So how do you develop these qualities in order to be completely magnetic not only in your leadership but in every other area of your life? Well, I've got 3 important steps to get you started.

Step One: Know who you REALLY are. When was the last time you sat down and asked yourself who you really are WITHOUT all of the titles, labels, deadlines, schedules, etc. of your busy life? If you were to strip away being a parent, brother, sister, friend, employee, mentor, or whatever else consumes your days, what would you be left with? What is it that lives at the base of your core, underneath all of the other stuff? This is what you want to uncover. See if you can create a list of qualities that define who you really are, and I challenge you to do it without labeling yourself in the process. This way you can discover characteristics (or what we call "ways of being" in the coaching space) about yourself that you get to hold onto and connect with every day. For example I'm loving, passionate, loyal, committed, energetic, inspiring, playful, creative, and generous. So... who are you?

Step Two: Learn to separate your WORTH from your results. This is a big one! I hate to break it to you, but you live in a society where most people think that if they constantly show up and do the work, then they will end up having all the things they've ever wanted. Unfortunately what this does is create a belief system that you have to "work hard to earn", and although that might be true in some situations, it is absolutely NOT true when it comes to your worth and your value. Here is an important message I really want you to know. Take a moment to read this very slowly to yourself, and allow it to sink in: YOUR WORTH EXISTS ALL ON ITS OWN. Now read that again. Your worth exists separate from your results, separate from your work, separate from your family, friends, and the people around you. You don't have to do anything to earn it. When you're able to allow this knowledge to consume your heart and lead your life, you will by default stop "performing", and will begin showing up as the powerful badass that you are.

Step Three: Make sure your internal matches your external. Have you ever tried to drive a car that's out of alignment? If so, you'll find that it tends to wobble all over the place when you're heading down the road, making it very difficult to get to where you're going. The same can be said for you, and the way you live your life. If there isn't alignment between the way you feel on the inside, and the way you're showing up on the outside, it's going to make it that much harder for you to be seen and heard. So I'm going to ask you a series of questions that might seem silly, but I really want you to think about: Does your appearance match your personality, or are you wearing clothing you're not really comfortable in? Are you listening to empowering music that inspires you to be your best, or are the songs filled with anger and rage? What about the shows you're watching, the places you're going, and the friends you communicate with? I ask these questions because I want you to realize that inconsistency creates inauthenticity. If you want to truly be irresistible, you get to create an environment around you that supports you in showing up that way. You get to be the same person in private that you are in public. You get to own who you are in every single way.

Finally, I want to remind you that learning to show up as the truest version of yourself takes time, practice, and trust. It can be scary to fully embrace who you are in a world that tells you "who you should be". If you find that you need additional support along the way, don't hesitate to reach out to me at www.ahigherwayofliving.com. I've also attached a FREE Confidence Hypnosis Audio to this article to support you in your journey! Just scan the QR code attached! or connect with me at http://www.ahigherwayofliving.com

Remember, you are one of a kind and absolutely worth it!
Amy

A HIGHER WAY OF LIVING

FREE Confidence
Hypnosis Audio

PMS, PERIODS, CRAVINGS...OH MY!

BY DR ELISABETH WYGANT

Does anyone else experience those fun PMS symptoms like bloating, breast tenderness, serious cramping, and intense mood swings? I know I used to (insert hand-raising emoji)! We've been told all of our lives that these symptoms that accompany our monthly period are just "part of being a woman" and that "we shouldn't have eaten the apple" because somehow our girl Eve has "cursed" us for all eternity. What if I told you, sis, that these engrained thoughts are flat out WRONG!? What if I told you that your period is sacred and does not have to be associated with impending doom every month? What if I told you, you are not meant to suffer every month and that you do NOT have to accept these symptoms as "normal," even though we are told they are "common." It's time to rewrite our narrative ladies and discover how absolu-FREAKIN-lutely incredible our bodies are!

Let's start at the beginning, our body practices the art of a delicate dance between all of its hormones. For this discussion, we will focus on estrogen and progesterone when it comes to hormone health. The PMS symptoms described above indicate there is some sort of imbalance occurring in these hormones themselves and can be solved by nurturing your body through holistic measures. In order to level them out, it's important to consider working with your body in a cyclical pattern instead of against it. Our current model for society is based on a 24-hour hustle and grind, which mimics the male hormone cycle, and consequently leads to us ladies riding on the struggle bus until we fizzle out. It's imperative that we take a look at the fabulous female hormonal cycle to end the story of total burnout and empower a generation of young women to step into their intuitive, empathetic, and intelligent nature.

Ladies, we operate on much more sophisticated clocks. Yes, you read that correctly we have more than one clock that determines our hormonal cycle. We have our 24-hour circadian rhythm that regulates metabolism, sleep, elimination, and production of specific hormones; but also what's called the infradian clock! The infradian clock is linked to your menstrual cycle and starts at puberty then ends at about fifty years old; it encompasses the four phases of a woman's cycle: menstrual, follicular, ovulatory, and luteal. The two clocks work closely together to optimize your overall health, when one is out of balance the other will soon tip the scales one way or the other.

"Now, how do we navigate the benefits of this newfound clock and what do we need to do to nurture it? "

If there is an imbalance in your 24-hour clock you might experience mood disorders, gut dysregulation, and reduced ability to think! If your circadian rhythm is off you could experience issues with irregular periods and longer menstrual cycles (your infradian rhythm). Now on the contrary, if your infradian rhythm is out of whack (hormonal irregularities) it can cause issues with your circadian rhythm like sleep issues, inability to regulate body temperature, and an irregular heart rate. This is why it's so important to be attuned to your body and understand your fifth vital sign, your period.

Now, how do we navigate the benefits of this newfound clock and what do we need to do to nurture it? Don't worry, I'm here to be your guide! We are going to chat about my favorite topic to balance that beautiful body to get out of hormonal chaos and into hormonal harmony; that's nutrition! Think about each phase of your cycle as a way to begin eating seasonally and cyclically. By doing so you are going to level up your hormonal advantage and begin to see a dramatic improvement in PMS symptoms. Check it out below:

- Follicular; hormone levels should be on the rise, but still need some TLC! Add foods that will bring you energy (think light and bright foods); gluten-free rolled oats, fermented foods (kimchi and sauerkraut) barley, carrots, parsley, broccoli, avocado, lemon, orange, lentils, ground flaxseeds, pumpkin seeds, cage-free chicken, organic free-range eggs, crab, almond butter, olives, apple cider vinegar.

- Ovulatory; estrogen is in full swing, your energy should be high, and your moods should be balanced. Because your body is running full speed ahead, think about adding foods that cool you down internally. Raw foods are your best choice in this arena; quinoa, red bell peppers, tomatoes, leafy greens, scallions, coconut, raspberry, strawberry, lentils, ground flaxseeds, pistachios, wild-caught salmon, tuna, shrimp, dark chocolate, coffee, and turmeric.

- Luteal; are you hungrier than usual a few days before your period? There's a reason for that and that's because during this phase you are gearing up for menstruation or pregnancy. Your body actually NEEDS more food to support this metabolic process. Sugar cravings actually come from a lack of stabilized blood sugar levels so eat those complex carbs throughout the day; sweet potatoes, jasmine rice, pumpkin, squash, cucumber, ginger, green apple, dates, chickpeas, sesame seeds, walnuts, grass-fed beef, cod, and peppermint.

- Menstrual; your hormones are at the lowest point during this phase, but there are ways to optimize this slump. Protein and healthy fats are essential to do so! Healthy fats maintain progesterone levels and aid in ovulation for your next cycle and protein contains amino acids that are required to create hormones entirely. Foods like wild rice, beets, kale, mushrooms, blueberry, watermelon, kidney beans, ground flaxseeds, pumpkin seeds, duck, grass-fed beef, venison, sushi nori, crab, lobster, and miso.

Start tracking your hormonal phase today and begin to implement these nutrient sources right away! An easy way to start is by going with your menstrual phase or your most troublesome phase (usually those with serious PMS symptoms start with luteal). Girlfriend, you've totally got this, it's time to kiss those cramps goodbye!

Want to find out which of your hormones are out of balance? Check out my fun personality quiz: Are Your Hormones Happy?

Connect with Dr. Elisabeth Wygant:
https://linktr.ee/ElisabethWygantWellness

Personality Quiz:
Are your Hormones Happy?

Meet Dr. Wygant

A CRITICAL HORMONE FOR FERTILITY: PROGESTERONE

BY DR. AUMATMA SIMMONS

> *Have you ever wanted to make a change in your diet, home, beauty routine, and/or mindset but were too overwhelmed with where to start?*

Progesterone is extremely essential during the childbearing years, if you don't produce enough progesterone, you may have trouble getting or staying pregnant. Many women are focused on progesterone during their fertile years but may be misled to believe that simply supplementing progesterone is going to support fertility.

What is progesterone? How is it made?

Progesterone is a hormone primarily secreted by the corpus luteum, the shell of the egg after the egg has been released from the ovary during ovulation. Progesterone is a crucial hormone in the luteal phase of the menstrual cycle, as well as the first trimester of pregnancy. Without sufficient and sustained production of progesterone, luteal phase defects, implantation, as well as early pregnancy loss.

The pituitary controls a hormone called Luteinizing hormone which will support the development of follicles that develop into potential eggs to be ovulated, and the interrelated corpus luteum that will produce progesterone for the luteal phase which may. When the egg is released from the ovary, the corpus luteum is left behind to produce progesterone for the 10-14 days post-ovulation. In addition, small amounts of progesterone are produced by the ovaries and adrenal glands.

Low progesterone may cause irregular or absent menstrual cycles, mood changes (particularly anxiety or depression), hot flashes, night sweats, vaginal dryness, and headaches or migraines in women who aren't pregnant. Pregnant women need progesterone to maintain their uterus until the baby is born. If progesterone levels are too low from the start or suddenly drop off during the first 10-12 weeks of pregnancy, the uterus may not be able to sustain the pregnancy, leading to spotting and miscarriage.

Many women have been led to believe that supplementation of progesterone pre-pregnancy and in the first trimester will lead to a healthy baby. However, without addressing the root causes of why progesterone might below to begin with bypasses the underlying problems, which may be too challenging to compensate for by a mere supplementation.

What are the root causes of low progesterone?

The biggest underlying factor is egg quality. Since the progesterone is primarily made by the corpus luteum of the egg that has been ovulated, the progesterone level is a direct reflection of the quality of the egg. If egg quality is low, several things may be helpful to consider.

First, appropriate restoring and optimizing of nutrients in the body. Many popular supplements are considered to be excellent to support egg quality. However, in my years of experience, I have noticed that even with the most popular supplements for egg quality, some women do not see the expected outcomes. I believe the reason for this is they may be deficient in critical nutrients that are not as "popular" but still have a significant impact on egg quality. Below I will share all of the key nutrients to support progesterone production.

Second, is the factor of stress. Although there is no 'direct' impact on progesterone, there is a noticeable difference in luteal phase length in cycles of stress. There is also a direct impact on pituitary hormones involved in the production of the egg. Too many of these hormones will affect egg quality, and hence progesterone levels.

What are the key nutrients to support progesterone production?

1. Vitamin B6. A study pooled a group of women who's having premenstrual tension syndrome, originally higher estrogen and lower progesterone levels to start the study. After supplementation of 200-800mg of vitamin B6 per day, results showed that the women had decreased their estrogen blood levels and increased their progesterone levels. (PMID: 6684167)

2. Vitamin D. The vitamin acts as a hormone in the body and can help regulate menstruation, increasing ovulation and progesterone levels. Also most bioavailable when you get it from sun exposure. (PMID: 30423869)

3. Vitamin E. Helps to clear excess estrogen in the body which will cause progesterone levels to be more optimal in proportion to estrogen. In addition, research has found

that vitamin E is uptaken by the corpus luteum and hence will have an impact on egg quality. (PMID: 16091003, PMID: 16091003)

4. Vitamin C. Vitamin C supplementation was associated with higher progesterone levels in perimenopausal women. This is significant because perimenopausal women usually have lower levels of progesterone naturally. (PMID: 26581679)

5. Vitamin B12. Can also regulate hormone levels and the internal stress response. Vitamin B12 influences the clearance of homocysteine in the blood. Homocysteine is an amino acid produced when proteins are broken down, but at elevated levels, it is called hyperhomocysteinemia which is damaging. These high levels are not good for the body because it can degrade the arterial lining, and increase stress levels. Increased stress levels have a negative effect on hormone balance, including progesterone. Due to this, vitamin B12 is one of the vitamins to increase progesterone. (PMID: 28545069)

It is important to note that although we have listed nutrients for progesterone, there are also two major food groups that are essential to progesterone production:

Essential fatty acids and complex unprocessed carbohydrates. The deficiency or restriction imposed by many diets in relation to these foods can sometimes challenge progesterone production. So, if you're considering dietary restrictions prior to pregnancy, please talk to a skilled Naturopathic Doctor or nutritionist before trying a fad diet.

Connect with Dr. Aumatma Simmons: https://linktr.ee/draumatma

Holistic Fertility
Cheat Sheat

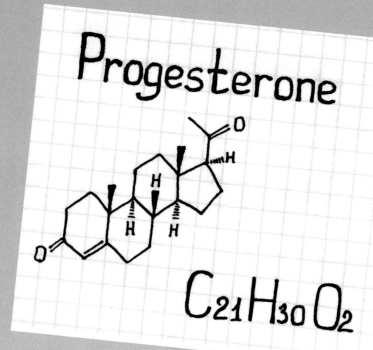

Progesterone

$C_{21}H_{30}O_2$

FINISHING 2022 STRONG THROUGH HABIT-STACKING

BY BRITTINIE WICK

Can you believe the year is half over!? Millions of people make resolutions to improve their lives every year, but more than 80% of those people give up on their goals. It's time to make July your new January, reflect on the goals you set earlier this year, and plan for the rest of the year.

To continue moving towards your goals - and the life you want - you need to look behind you to see what has worked well and what has not worked well in the past.

You want to be able to identify where and why you were successful so that you can replicate it. And on the flip side, you need to be able to identify where you went astray in previous endeavors so that you can avoid being waylaid by those same obstacles.

This is not about white-knuckling and disciplining yourself towards your goals. Instead, let's focus on taking intentional, deliberate action that works with your lifestyle, adds real value to your quality of life, gets you excited about the future, and steadily moves you closer to your own personal vision of success.

Let's start with the end in mind. Close your eyes for a minute (after you finish reading this section!). It's December 31st, 2022. You're sitting down with a friend for a delicious glass of wine, and you're looking back over the year. You're thinking about how PROUD of yourself you are for everything you've accomplished, pushing yourself out of your comfort zone, and living the year with INTENTION. You feel fulfilled, at peace, excited about the future, and SUCCESSFUL in the important areas of your life. Things like your relationships, health, and fitness, career, personal growth, finances, etc.

What does success look like in those areas for YOU? And when I say "YOU," I'm not talking about how other people would define success. I'm talking about how YOU would define it and what that truly would look like for you. One important thing to remember is that "success" doesn't always mean you've "arrived." But it DOES mean you're happy with your progress in a certain period of time.

Now let's take that first step.

It's time to scan your list and think about the HABITS you'll need to develop in your daily routine to move you closer to your vision of success. You do NOT have to overhaul your entire life with a dozen new habits! When you're coming up with your own habits, it's important to keep them realistic. These can (and will) be habits that expand over time – adding time, energy, and resources as they become more ingrained into your daily routine. Starting small and achieving daily and weekly wins will help you build momentum so that you'll be able to FOLLOW-THROUGH and CRUSH your goals this year, For example, If your vision of success is reaching a specific health goal, your habit could be twice-weekly meal prep or prioritizing four workouts a week.

Action: Take a look at your vision of success for health and wellness for the rest of 2022 and come up with six results-driven habits that you can add to your life, one for each month. Remember to keep them simple and achievable– this is key!! Once you have your six new habits, it's time to decide the ORDER you want to tackle them. If you try to install too many new habits at once, you're setting yourself up for overwhelm and failure. We'll start with just ONE in July and continue adding ONE new habit every month for the rest of the year. This approach may take a little longer, but it is SO worth it because you won't be setting the same goals again next year, as most people will in January 2023! Start with the habits you feel most excited about and give you the highest reward. When you do this, you'll get quick wins that will help you stay motivated and give you a big shot of results right out of the gate! Remember, make sure the habit is REALISTIC – something you actually have TIME for without creating a big disruption in your daily life.

For example, going from zero workouts a week to 6 hour-long workouts a week is probably not realistic, but making time for shorter and/or less frequent workouts IS realistic.

You can always add later on as you become more proficient. The key is to motivate yourself forward toward SUCCESS with SUCCESS! Each month you will ADD a new habit, so in July, you will start with one habit. In August, you'll stack another habit and continue until December. Then by the end of the year, you have added six new success-creating habits to your life! How to implement: write down your new habit for the month

and how many times you will do it each week. Write down your "why" – why is this habit so important to you? Why are you including it as a success habit? Then track your progress by making a BIG "X" or color in the circle on the date you complete your habit in a tracker/calendar. Do NOT skip this step. Looking back on all that you have accomplished can motivate you forward.

Remember, it's the JOURNEY – the daily actions you take - where the true success lives. Let's finish 2022 STRONG!!

Connect with Brittinie Wick: https://linktr.ee/bawick19

Grab Brittinie's "Healthy at Every Age" guide! Watch a preview!

BASIC SKIN TIPS
FOR GLOWING SKIN

BY RACHEL VARGA BSCN, RN, CANS

With summer just around the corner, what can we do to get our skin ready for a little more exposure of our arms and legs and more glowing and radiant skin? Let's talk about body skin care which is essentially simply an extension of what you can do for the face, eyelids, neck, chest, and hands but to carry onwards and downwards to the arms, back, abdomen and legs!

Let's start with the 5 basics for healthy skin which include cleansing, moisturizing, sun protection, exfoliation, and weekly masks and peels. Ensuring that you are cleansing the skin morning and night is key in order to cleanse off dirt, oil, debris, pollution, cosmetic creams, and makeup in the evening and then again in the morning. Taking a bath or shower before bed is a great strategy to ensure your skin is clean for 7-8 hours while your body (and skin) are regenerating. By cleansing the skin we are literally rinsing off debris from the skin that is creating oxidative stress which is in fact contributing to cellular aging and skin aging as inflammation is a root cause of aging. With this being said, it is not necessary to scrub and apply soap to the entire body, but do use a cleanser am and pm for the face, neck, and chest, but a rinse to the rest of the body is perfect. You may want to use a simple homemade castile soap with your favorite essential oils such as clary sage, rose, or lavender. Frankincense and peppermint can be a bit irritating or too stimulating to the skin in the evening if used in the bath so use these sparingly.

Moisturizing the skin morning and night is like giving your skin the multivitamins that it needs to feed it on a cellular level as the skin is our largest organ. I recommend a practitioner/medical grade moisturizer packed with antioxidants and peptides for the face, eyelids, neck and chest, and you can go for a more locally made type of body product for moisturizing. It's important to always ensure that your skin care and personal care products are free of parabens, phthalates, artificial dyes, fragrances and isn't tested on animals. If you're not sure where to start simply book your One on One session and it will be my pleasure to guide you through your at-home and in-clinic routine.

Sun protection is key. I have worked with thousands of clients since 2011 and many of my clients say they don't wear sunscreen every day because they aren't in the sun every day. This is a bit of a catch 22 as the LED lighting in our home emits a type of blue light that in fact reaches about three times deeper into the skin than the UVA and UVB rays from the outdoor natural sunlight. Many of us are working from home or in an office setting in front of computer screens and wearing daily SPF protection is key to reduce cellular aging and oxidative damage which leads to things like collagen and elastin breakdown and sun or age spots. Skin cancer is also very real and it is important that we protect the largest organ of our bodies and take notice of new lesions that arise and have them promptly looked at by a Physician. The key with sunscreen use is to only use a mineral-based sunscreen like zinc or titanium dioxide. Many sunscreens, makeup, tinted moisturizers and primers are a blend of mineral and chemical sunscreen filters and research shows that chemical sunscreen

filters do in fact create DNA damage and oxidative cellular stress as seen in marine life studies. Some chemical-based sunscreen filters are also known hormone disruptors and should be completely avoided. If you're not sure if your sunscreen is safe, simply look at the label and find the medicinal/active ingredients section and if anything else other than zinc or titanium are listed, then those are chemical filters and the product should be discarded or not purchased in the first place. Some places like Hawaii and Australia are already starting to ban the importation of chemical sunscreen filters because of the damage on coral reefs which also damages our human biology.

Exfoliation is an aspect of skin health that is often overlooked or bypassed if someone believes they have sensitive or reactive skin. Actually, exfoliation is key in order to gently remove the top layer of the skin called the stratum corneum which up close looks like corn flakes and are in fact dead cells. When these dead cells pile on top of one another they can trap dirt, oil, debris, beauty products and make up and in fact, can contribute to oxidative damage to the skin which is why cleansing and exfoliating is important so that the skin cells can breathe and can absorb fresh nutrients like in a potent antioxidant and peptide-rich moisturizer to feed and nourish the skin every AM and PM. The trick with exfoliation is to use a product that isn't jagged or crystalline in nature which can in fact create microtears into the skin and can in fact contribute to skin sensitivity and irritation.

With the products you already have that don't have those ingredients, you can make a few tweaks to your product routine and application by following and downloading my free Sophisticated Skin Cheat Sheet where I cover my top 5 basics of what you need to know in regards to cleansing, moisturizing, sun protection, exfoliation and weekly peels or masks. I also would love to share with you my Rejuvenation Planning Guide which is like a daytime planner and budgeting tool with pre/post recovery tips for your rejuvenation journey! These are completely free tools that I know will help get you started on the right track to optimizing what you're already doing and then reach out when you're ready to receive customized One on One guidance with me at https://RachelVarga.ca/ Use promo code BestHolisticLife for 15% off of your One on One call with me at https://RachelVarga.ca/get-started and it will be my pleasure to help guide you through aging impossibly well for many years to come!

Many thanks and be well,
Rachel Varga, BScN, RN, CANS, Board Certified Aesthetic Nurse Specialist since 2011

Host of The Rachel Varga Podcast and The Rachel Varga YouTube Channel
Learn more at https://RachelVarga.ca

RACHEL VARGA

NATURALLY A
Goddess

CONSUMER PRODUCTS UNCOVERED

BY CHRISTINA SILVEIRA

What is going on in that head of yours and what are you saying to yourself?

Would we be shocked to know?

It's a gorgeous summer morning and you're starting to settle into your outdoor Zen zone. You hear the birds chirping, there is a gentle breeze, the sun is rising and embracing your face like a warm hug. You're about to start your daily meditation. All of a sudden, you begin to smell a very strong aroma that interrupts your focus and you wonder what has thrown off your focus. Unfortunately what you are smelling is not the aroma of the magnificent flowers you have growing in your garden. It is the smell of your neighbor's laundry after using a heavily scented laundry detergent and dryer sheets.

The environments in which we live in and utilize the most are our homes and cars. But did you ever stop to think about what is in your immediate environment that could be lurking where it doesn't belong? It's incredible to think that the air inside our homes is 200-300 times more toxic than the air we breathe outside. When I started my journey into a non-toxic living environment, I was shocked and overwhelmed by the number of toxins and chemicals that were hidden in common everyday household items we used. These products include cleaning products, candles and air fresheners, body care products, hair care products, skin products, cosmetics, laundry products, and furniture. We typically don't give a second thought to a simple task like washing our clothes, but that overpowering scent of laundry detergent and dryer sheets actually contains some of the most harmful chemicals and toxins around.

Our skin is the body's largest organ, so it would make sense that everything we are putting on our skin and breathing in, gets absorbed and enters our bloodstream. This then travels to all of our major organs. When we continuously use products that contain harmful ingredients, we are disturbing and suppressing our body's natural abilities to detox. Over time, our body will begin to give us clues that our body is becoming more toxic and in need of change. Some indicators are skin irritations, sudden respiratory concerns, sudden allergies, autoimmune disorders, organ malfunctions, hormone imbalances, sudden difficulties sleeping and our overall mental wellbeing has been affected. However, if we ignore these clues, our body will reach its tipping point and tip into a state of illness and dis-ease.

As women, we tend to use a lot more products than our male counterparts. In a single day, the average woman uses sixty to eighty products per day. This equates to upwards of fifty thousand chemicals within a twenty-four-hour period. This wouldn't be a cause for concern if the products we were using were completely natural. However, because the FDA does not regulate cosmetics, it is very easy for companies to use green-washing marketing techniques to disguise ingredients or classify them under an umbrella term. Consumers are being misled into believing a product is beneficial to them when in reality they are causing increasingly more harm to our overall wellness. For example, there are thousands of individual ingredients that can be used to formulate a product, and only a handful of these are banned for use in consumer products. The majority of the ingredients used to make these formulations that most of us had come to love are actually, in fact, harmful to our bodies in more ways than most of us are aware of. There is a long list of ingredients that are a cause for concern. Some of the more known ones include SLS, SLES, Phthalates, Oxybenzone, Formaldehyde, and fragrances or perfumes. The latter is perhaps the most known ingredient because it is in nearly every product on the market. In fact, the term fragrance or perfume should be labeled as 'hidden chemicals' because it contains over three thousand chemicals alone.

Making the transition to non-toxic & green products can be completely overwhelming and seem like too much work. I recommend taking things slowly, starting with one small change, and continuing to build on what you've previously done. Do your own research so you can make your own decisions about what is best for you and your family! Here are some suggestions on making it affordable and enjoyable:

Start by swapping one product at a time. It is best to start with the product you use the most often, such as cleaning supplies, air fresheners, deodorant, lotion, hair care, and cosmetics. Read the labels and look up each ingredient.

1. Start by making one green product yourself to replace a harmful one in your home, and notice how you start to feel and notice things differently.

2. Decide where you draw your line. Do your own research and decide what ingredients in what amounts you are comfortable with. Use the resources around you to make an informed decision.

3. Be aware of companies using greenwashing marketing techniques from bigger corporations. Instead, opt into purchasing from local artisans.

4. Research how to make your own products and DIY. Being as self-sufficient as possible is such an empowering feeling!

No matter where you are on your journey of green and non-toxic beauty and home care, the best tool you can have in your pocket is knowledge. You are empowering yourself and your family to make better choices. You are leading by example and taking charge of your own life. When we know better, we do better.

Connect with Christina Silverira: linktr.ee/naturallyagoddess

Top 5 Most Asked for Green Cleaning Recipes

ASK DANIELLE

Danielle, I have so many goals but I find myself procrastinating. How do I stop sabotaging myself so I can move forward?

Hey Christine!

First your goals cant be that great if you are postponing taking action to make them a reality. I'd take inventory of how you might be limiting yourself and your goals because you are scared to fail before you even begin. You might also have a goal that is too far in the future and you just can't relate to the image of your future self that has succeeded!

First, rethink your goals. Make sure you are not shrinking the goal because it's something you " think" you can be, do or have. A worthy goal is one that makes you jump out of bed in the morning and you spend time with every day. Like a new lover, you get excited every time you bring the image to mind. Next tap into the version of you when the wish is fulfilled. Who are you, what old do you believe, who do you hang out with, what do you wear, where do you live, what are your habits, what is different about this up-leveled version of you? Most importantly, you are your own hero; no one is coming to save you and no one is going to stoke the fire within you. You need to dig deep into why you want what you want in the first place. Once you clear out the old beliefs that are blocking you from taking inspired and aligned action you will stop procrastination and start mobbing toward the direction of your dreams with gusto.

I feel like my life is really hard. I try harder, work more, and yet nothing comes easy. I'm always stressed and can't seem to catch a break! Help! xo Noxi

Hi Noxi!

The idea that life is hard and is happening TO YOU is a victim consciousness and is the root of what needs to be healed. While your life may have been difficult, as adults we get to choose how we live and how we think. Working harder and more is not the answer to your problems. You need to learn how to BE and how to THINK as someone who lives life with ease. This may require you to make different choices in your work, relationships, and health and wellness habits. The Law of Polarity one of the Universal laws says that the opposite of what we are experiencing is available to us. That means if you are living in " hard" " easy " is also available. Adding a good dose of gratitude into your day and making new decisions that support your new easeful lifestyle will create new experiences and doors opening to this new up-leveled YOU.

Our body patterns can be wired for struggle. When we are wired for the struggle we are typically living in a state of fight/flight/freeze/fawn. These states become a typical place for us to be in our system and with others. How do you know if you're in this place? Think back to a time when you had a great morning- relaxed, calm, joyful even. Your day was filled with possibility and potential. Then something happened to shake you out of that state. Maybe on your way to work, you were in a fender bender or you spilled nuclear hot coffee all over your white dress or got pulled over and got a speeding ticket. You most likely dipped into this dysregulated state at least temporarily. The issue comes when we are in a dysregulated state all of the time and we struggle with feeling regulated described by some as grounded, centered, ease, peace and calm. If you discover upon reflection that you are dysregulated - feeling consistent stress, in your monkey mind, disconnected from yourself and others, anxious, angry, feeling heavy on the shoulders with responsibility and overwhelm then you may choose to take some time each day to practice being in a regulated state. I have a free tool called Somatic Practices that helps others access this regulated state so feel free to grab that on my Instagram @daniellemarggraf.

Life doesn't have to be a struggle. The same berry it takes to stay in struggle is the same amount of energy to be at ease.

Link: https://daniellemarggraf.taplink.ws/

Bio:

Danielle Marggraf is a leader in the feminine wealth movement. Followed by women worldwide for her inspiring and no-nonsense teaching style, Danielle mixes her spiritual badassery with money and nervous system coach training for women with nervous system healing practices to literally rewire your body for more freedom, fulfillment and feminine financial flow.

Her programs of all levels transform women in their business and personal lives. She is an activator for women to be wealthy and worthy banishing shame from their body systems and growing lucrative, soul-enriching businesses as well as understanding that their bank accounts and their lives are a reflection of their body patterns.

As a result, graduates of Danielle's wealth consciousness programs quickly begin to massively uplevel their income, let go of past money blocks, and experience deep, soul-level breakthroughs in claiming their worth, connecting to their wisdom and up-leveling energetically so they prosper in every area of their lives.

THE "IT'S FINE FACTOR"

BY JUDY HAHN

Stress. We recognize it easily when we think of experiences with lack of finances, being overly busy, watching/witnessing or living through distressing events, and experiencing unpleasant life disruptions such as job loss. However, there are other things – small things – that cause us to stress much more frequently than we realize but we don't recognize or pay much attention to them. Why? Because we haven't formed an accepting relationship with them! Sounds crazy, right? Accepting a relationship with stress of any kind seems like the most illogical thing ever. Yet each of us does exactly that in one way or another, daily, and its impact on our health can be troublesome.

To make this easier to understand, let's call the illogical relationships that we've formed with "small things" stress as the, "It's fine factor." Why give it a name? Because these "accepted relationships" are often unnoticed, misunderstood, and hiding right before our very eyes. We go on with them for so long that sometimes we don't even realize that our body or mind is warning us that it's under stress. So, putting a name to these "little things" can help us recognize and realize our personal patterns.

Here's how it happens: The "It's Fine Factor" is lurking in the little things that we have learned to live with. Things such as a continually noisy environment, a horribly uncomfortable desk chair, unseen toxins/allergens, or poor lighting where we read the most.   We may even be in a relationship where abuse/manipulation has become so expected that we are no longer aware of just how stressful that behavior is. We go on telling ourselves that "it's fine" yet our brains and bodies are reacting to the effects of these stressors continually. If you think about what you've been living with that falls under the "It's Fine Factor" you may begin to recognize the patterns in how your body has been responding. You may experience tension headaches, or worse, migraines. Maybe your doctor has been warning you of high blood pressure or high cholesterol. You may not be sleeping well – or needing much more sleep than average. You may be either over or under eating and you may get sick frequently. Does any of this sound familiar? Most likely, everyone can say, "Yes, in the past." Unfortunately, a large majority of us can respond, "Yes, right now."

WHY we live with a large list under the "It's Fine Factor" is the result of many things. It could be societal conditioning or the way our parents raised us. We could be so distracted by daily life that we aren't paying attention. Or, so detached from ourselves that we don't feel "worthy" of removing ourselves from the stress-causing situations. It could be a combination of some or all of these things. No matter the why, I'm here to tell you that you can – and should – no longer accept a relationship with "small" stressors.

Here are some simple steps to start:

1. Take a look at your life and see where you've been accepting a relationship with stress.
2. Write the list and leave it just as it is for 24 hours.
3. Either in another column or on another page, write down how you've been feeling both physically and emotionally.
4. Go back to both lists after 24 hours and add if you need to.
5. Read it all out loud. How are you feeling as you read it? Write this down.
6. Now, assess what changes you'll need to make so the list becomes as small as possible. -
7. Imagine that anything you need to do that will make the list small IS possible.
8. Take action!

For some people, the last item on that list isn't hard at all. But for others, the changes may seem impossible because you may not know where to start. This is perfectly OK and you should be proud of yourself for knowing that you'll benefit from help.

Here's the deal; as a Functional Medicine Wellness Coach, I understand that most of my clients are coming to me with symptoms related to stress even if they don't know it themselves. Because I seek the root cause(s) of dis-ease, I can help my clients to see their relationship to stress and its impact on their physical and emotional health in a new light. By creating a customized plan focused on their specific concerns, the impossible becomes very possible. I hear you, there's no doubt that change is hard – breaking habits is even harder. But with the right support, I've witnessed incredibly positive changes in my clients because they finally decided to invest in themselves. You can too! Finding the right help for your needs will take from feeling "It's fine...." to feeling fabulous!

Connect with Judy Hahn:
https://taplink.cc/theguthealthgeek

Free Functional Medicine Video Series

Meet Judy

Hahn
Holistic
Health

10 MINUTE CORE CHALLENGE

WORKOUT WITH BRITTINIE WICK

Many people associate the core with an image of toned 6-pack abs, but that is an incomplete picture.

Our core is actually comprised of over 30 different muscles. There are deep muscles that surround the spinal cord (keeping us upright), internal and external obliques, the outer "abs", the glutes, and back muscles.

Strengthening and stabilizing the core is incredibly important, especially for women who've had children.

You may also need to focus on your core if you suffer from lower back pain, poor posture, incontinence, and/or weakness in your extremities, so try this 10-minute core challenge!

10 minute core challenge

Do the following 10 exercises for 45 seconds each, taking 15 seconds to recover between exercises

Jackknife (Right Leg Extended)
Bicycle crunches
Jackknife (Left Leg Extended)
Superman
Oblique crunches (Right Side)
Plank
Oblique crunches (Left Side)
Reverse crunches
Side plank with dip (Right Side)
Side plank with dip (Left Side)

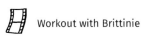
Workout with Brittinie

JACKKNIFE

Lie on your back with one leg extended out and one knee in towards your chest. Raise your extended leg about 2 inches off the floor and hold in this position.

Crunch repeatedly with your hands crossed over your chest keeping both legs off the ground. Switch legs and repeat on the other side. When it is time to switch legs, make sure not to drop your legs to the floor.

BICYCLE CRUNCHES

Lie on your back with your elbows bent and your hands on either side of your head. Simultaneously bring your right knee in towards your chest while crunching up and rotating your torso to the right, attempting to touch your left elbow to the right knee. Keeping your core tight, extend your right leg while bringing in your left knee and crunching and rotating to touch it to your right elbow. Keep both feet off the ground for the duration of the exercise. Continue alternating sides for the desired number of reps or time. (Note: if extending your leg is challenging right now, keep your knee bent at a 90-degree angle throughout the exercise.)

SUPERMAN

Lie on your stomach in a prone position with your arms and legs extended out. Place a folded towel or mat underneath the pelvis to remove any pressure on the lower back during this exercise.

Simultaneously, raise your legs and arms off the floor and squeeze your glutes. Lower arms and legs back to the ground. Variations: Opposite arm with the opposite leg, arms only, legs only.

OBLIQUE CRUNCH

Lie on your upper back in a supine position with your knees and hips bent. Lower your legs to the left side at a 90° angle in the hip. Flex your waist to raise your upper torso a few inches off the ground while focusing your attention on the right oblique. Control the movement back down to the ground and repeat for the desired number of reps. Repeat on the right side.

PLANK

Lie on your stomach in a prone position with your legs extended out. Place your forearms (should be parallel) on the ground and move into a position similar to the top of a "push-up" except you are on your forearms and not your hands. With your feet together, push out strong through your heels, with your shoulders stable. Keep your core tight, back flat, and your tailbone tucked. Hold this position for the desired amount of time.

REVERSE CRUNCHES

Lie on your back with your hands underneath the top of your glutes to support your lower back. Keep your neck relaxed and on the ground throughout the movement. Keep your legs slightly bent and flex the waist and hips to raise your legs up to the sky using your core to perform the movement. Control the movement back to the starting position and repeat.

Note: this exercise can also be done with the knees bent to 90 degrees.

SIDE PLANK
(WITH AND WITHOUT A DIP)

Lie on your left side with your legs together. Place your left forearm on the ground with your left elbow directly underneath your left shoulder. Press through your shoulder to elevate your entire body to a side plank keeping your feet stacked. Hold. For the dip: Simply lower your hips to the ground and raise them back up to the top of the side plank. Repeat this motion for the desired number of reps. Keep your core tight, back flat, and your tailbone tucked. Repeat on the right side for the desired amount of time.

FOR YOUR EYES

FAVORITE BOOKS

Unclutter Your Soul by Trina McNeilly

We all want our lives to change for the better—to become the healthiest versions of ourselves in spirit, soul, and body. Yet we still struggle. Author Trina McNeilly, looking for order in her own life, embarked on an inward journey to the home of her heart and soul to find healing and health from the inside out.

https://www.amazon.com/Unclutter-Your-Soul-Overcome-Overwhelms/dp/078525000X/r

Find Your People: Building Deep Community in a Lonely World by Jennie Allen

In a world that's both more connected and more isolating than ever before, we're often tempted to do life alone, whether because we're so busy or because relationships feel risky and hard. But science confirms that consistent, meaningful connection with others has a powerful impact on our well-being. We are meant to live known and loved. But so many are hiding behind emotional walls that we're experiencing an epidemic of loneliness..

https://www.amazon.com/Find-Your-People-Building-Community/dp/0593193385/

Get Published by James Patrick

It is impossible to grow your fitness brand if no one knows you exist! That is why you need to tap into a proven system to grow your fitness, health or life coaching business by leveraging the power of media to amplify your authority and generate leads!

.

https://join.jamespatrick.com/getpublishedguide

Blue Zones by Dan Buettner

Bestselling author, longevity expert, and National Geographic Explorer Dan Buettner reports on health, fitness, diet, and aging, drawing on his research from extraordinarily long-lived communities--Blue Zones--around the globe. Buettner has launched a major public health initiative to transform cities based on principles from this book, an updated and expanded edition of his bestselling classic on longevity.

https://www.amazon.com/Blue-Zones-Second-Lessons-Longest-ebook/dp/B007WL6D60/ref

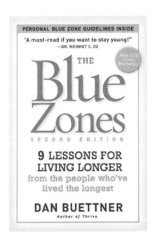

The Mind-Gut Connection: by Emeran Mayer, MD

Combining cutting-edge neuroscience with the latest discoveries on the human microbiome, a practical guide in the tradition of Wheat Belly and Grain Brain that conclusively demonstrates the inextricable, biological link between mind and body.

https://www.amazon.com/Mind-Gut-Connection-Conversation-Impacts-Choices/dp/0062376586/ref

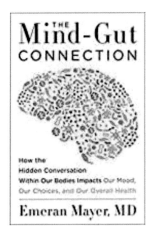

What if this Is the Fun Part? by Carolyn Freyer-Jones & Michelle Bauman

What if This Is the Fun Part? invites you into the realization that your life is yours to create, and you need never stop growing, living, and loving. "A funny, vulnerable, courageous book that will take you on a journey that evokes the real feelings of being human." ~ Stephen McGhee

https://www.amazon.com/What-this-Fun-Part-friendship/dp/1737947501/ref

WHAT AWAITS YOU IN AUGUST!

Made in the USA
Las Vegas, NV
06 May 2022

48534618R00071